A Mother's
Influence

Write Back Soon: Letters of Love and Encouragement to Young Women

A Mother's Influence

Margaret D. Nadauld

DESERET
BOOK
SALT LAKE CITY, UTAH

Words and music to "Remember the Children" are by Janice Kapp Perry and come from the album *In the Arms of His Love* (Provo: Prime Recordings, 1992). Used with permission.

Visit us at deseretbook.com

Library of Congress Cataloging-in-Publication Data

Nadauld, Margaret D., 1944-
  A mother's influence / Margaret D. Nadauld.
      p.   cm.
  Includes bibliographical references and index.
  ISBN 1-59038-239-0 (hardbound : alk. paper)
  1. Motherhood.   2. Motherhood—Religious aspects—Mormon Church.   3. Mothers.   4. Mothers—Religious life.   I. Title.
  HQ759.N273 2004
  248.8'431—dc22   2003027095

Printed in Canada   29359-7185
Friesens, Manitoba, Canada
10   9   8   7   6   5   4   3   2   1

For my dear husband, Stephen,
and our seven beloved sons
and their families,
who bring us great joy and rejoicing

FEAR THOU NOT; FOR I AM WITH THEE: BE NOT

DISMAYED; FOR I AM THY GOD: I WILL STRENGTHEN

THEE; YEA, I WILL HELP THEE; YEA, I WILL UPHOLD

THEE WITH THE RIGHT HAND OF MY RIGHTEOUSNESS.

ISAIAH 41:10

Contents

Contents

1

A Woman of Faith

Motherhood is awe-inspiring, there is no question about it. On that glorious day of days when your newborn child was placed in your arms, a sacred partnership was formed between you and God. Women of faith know this. What divine trust is placed in an ordinary woman as she is chosen to help nurture a child of God and thus help to shape a rising generation!

In times of doubt you may have wondered how you could adequately fulfill such an awesome responsibility. Add to that the charge given to us by an apostle of God, Elder M. Russell Ballard: "What we need now is the greatest generation of missionaries in the history of the Church. We need worthy, qualified, spiritually energized missionaries who, like Helaman's 2,000 stripling warriors, are 'exceedingly valiant for courage, and also for strength and activity' and who are 'true at all times in whatsoever thing they [are] entrusted' (Alma 53:20)."[1]

In order to fulfill this kind of a request, mothers are going to have to be like the legendary mothers of those stripling warriors, mothers whose faith was strong and who taught their children so well that their faith led them to extraordinary accomplishments. Those children did "not doubt [their] mothers knew it" (Alma 56:48).

There is no doubt about it, this kind of mothering requires that we be women of firm faith in the Lord Jesus Christ. Faith in Him helps us understand God's plan for each of His children. His great plan of happiness includes understanding that each spirit lived with God, the Eternal Father, and accomplished and learned and loved long before he or she came into our homes. It includes knowing that love and relationships and family go on forever, eternally.

I have often thought about Mary, the mother of Jesus, and how she fulfilled her divine calling to motherhood, knowing that her child was the literal Son of God. Think of her great faith and utter dependence on heavenly help! That divine help came for her, and I believe that it will likewise come for all mothers, personalized and fashioned just for you.

As I have sought to increase my faith I have read from the pages of sacred scripture. I treasure the teachings of the holy life of the Lord Jesus Christ. In my mind's eye I have watched Jesus as He "increased in wisdom and stature, and in favour with God and man" (Luke 2:52). In my reading, I was there when He raised the dead. He healed the sick, fed the five thousand, brought comfort and hope and a process for peace into the world that He had created. He forgave those who mocked and tortured and crucified Him—for they knew not what they did. I saw the divine love and concern He had for His mother, though He suffered in supreme agony Himself. He overcame death so that we can too. He has prepared a place for us in heaven with our Eternal Father. He has taught us the plan for happiness and given us the vision of it and the hope to follow it. His was the ultimate life of sacrifice and a life of service to fulfill the plan of God His Father.

A Latter-day Saint mother who follows Christ's example in her daily living begins to fulfill God's plan for her. By so doing she can be a powerful influence for good in the lives of her children, she can better cope in today's world and successfully meet the many and varied challenges of mortality. I have known such women and they have been a guiding light to me. The Latter-day Saint woman who follows Christ is a true Christian in the very best sense of the word. She is a woman of faith who *trusts God,* is *confident* and *fearless.*

A woman of faith trusts God and faces adversity with hope. She knows of His interest in her life. She knows that He knows her. She loves His words and drinks deeply of that living water. She is grateful for the prophet He has sent for these latter days and she trusts his counsel and follows it, for she knows that by so doing she will find safety and peace. In prayer she seeks the kind, unfaltering guidance and help of a listening Heavenly Father. As she prays she listens—allowing the communication to be two-way. She trusts that in His still and quiet way, He will "lead [her] by the hand, and give [her] answer to [her] prayers" (D&C 112:10).

A woman of faith is confident because she understands the divine plan of our Heavenly Father and her role to bless lives. She is confident that any sacrifice she makes is worth something in an eternal sense. She knows about sacrifice from knowing of the life of the Savior.

4

She knows that her sacrifices may be small by comparison, but she knows that Heavenly Father understands and values what she does to strengthen her home and family. Her confidence grows because she is virtuous and lovely and gracious, which is even better than being beautiful. She has pure motives. She is loving and gentle and kind. The heart of her husband and her children safely trust in her (see Proverbs 31:11), and so do the children or youth or women that she has been called to teach, lead, serve, and love. They are drawn to her because of the special spirit that she radiates. The image of God is in her countenance, and that is appealing and attractive and important (see Alma 5:14). She is confident that she is fashioning a character and a record of performance that will be invited to stand in the presence of her Heavenly Father. She will be able to do so with the sense that she fully belongs there, that she is known by Him and loved and valued and treasured forever and always.

A woman of faith is fearless. She fears no evil, for God is with her (see Psalm 23:4). There is no ambiguity, no uncertain trump in her life. She can live a principled life because she studies the doctrine and teachings of a perfect teacher, the Master. She is a noble example to all who know her. She is less than perfect, of course, not because she doesn't have perfect principles or the perfect example in Christ, but because she is human. She stays away from the evil influence and the unclean thing, and if it encroaches on her territory, she is as a lioness protecting her cubs.

A fearless woman of faith has the courage to talk with her children about practices that would destroy them. They not only *hear* her discuss her commitment, but they *see* her commitment in her daily living, in the way she dresses, in what she reads and watches, in how she spends her leisure, in what she loves and laughs at, in who she attracts, and in how she acts at all times, in all things, and in all places.

A woman of faith has a certain style of her own that is attractive and appealing and joyful and bright and good! She seeks out and promotes that which is uplifting and positive and happy.

Thank heaven for women of faith in our lives! I am forever grateful for the noble women of faith who have inspired me and shown me the way on my path of motherhood. These women of faith love the Lord. They want Him to know it by the life they live, by the words they speak, by the service they render to His children, by their every action. They know that He loves them even though they are imperfect and still trying to be better. They know that when they do their very best, that it is enough, as President Hinckley has told us.[2]

This little book is a collection of thoughts on motherhood. Each chapter is for the purpose of building your faith and trust and confidence and courage in raising the greatest generation the world has ever known. You *can* do this in spite of living in these troubled times. It is hoped that you will also feel a renewed happiness, a sense of humor, a zest and an enthusiasm for the daily-ness of mothering. And may you remember always the great and everlasting worth of your work.

2

The Family—
How Firm a Foundation

Occasionally it was like the Wild, Wild West in the foundation-building days of our family. Life was sometimes hectic as we tried to tame and civilize our little ones. One day I recorded in my journal some notes about the awesome task of building family foundations and what it was really like: "Got up early. Made German pancakes and hot oatmeal and juice. Practicing violin with James when a baby threw and shattered a glass. Cleaned it up and disciplined him. Fed the boys. Practiced piano with Lincoln while a little one wet on the kitchen floor and another emptied corn flakes on the bedroom floor, all the while Taylor was running wild throughout the house. Sent to room. Two phone calls—one to go visiting teaching and the other to borrow the boys' snow clothes. All this before 8 A.M. A typical day's beginning." At the end of the day, I recorded the question, "What kind of children and what kind of woman will emerge from this?"

With the perspective of years, it appears that the only thing to do was to just keep after it, every day. One day you may wake up and see that you have high school graduates, missionaries, college graduates, temple-married children who pay their tithing and their mortgages and serve others. And you will say, when did such a thing happen?

I love the wonderful hymn we often sing: "How firm a foundation, ye Saints of the Lord, is laid for your faith in his excellent word!"[1] I wonder if that is the song the pioneer workers sang as they tore up the weakening foundation laid for the Salt Lake Temple to replace it with firm and solid granite which would be enduring in strength and stand the test of time. With such determination to do it right and dedication to excellence, no wonder this magnificent structure took forty years to build.

You and I are today laying foundations that will outlast anything earthly, for we are building families— families dedicated to the work of God. We are building families that are the foundation of society and the foundation of the Church—families that will be enduring in strength and must withstand the tests of our time.

When considered in those terms, the task seems too monumental, too imposing, too grand for a mere mortal woman to tackle. But you are just the one to do it! And I am grateful for the honor of standing with you in these latter days as we put our collective hearts, minds, and very lives to the attention of this holy endeavor.

The teaching that mothers do takes great patience, a sense of humor, and love. And it takes consistent, never-ending effort to build a foundation that is steady and firm.

Every time a child kneels at a mother's knee to pray, the child is taught.

When going to church is the expected natural course of events each week, a child is taught.

When going to church is a pleasant event in the week for the family, a child is taught.

When classroom teachings are discussed at home, a child is taught, twice.

When home teachers are welcomed with appreciation, a child is taught.

When tithing is paid first and regarded as important, a child is taught.

When parents love the Lord and find joy in living His teachings, a child is taught.

When a parent repents and asks forgiveness of a child, a child is taught and then forgives and forgets.

When a parent honors marital vows with complete fidelity, a child is taught and feels safe.

When scriptures are part of teaching in the home, a child is taught, by the Spirit as well as by the word.

When a parent is seen reading for enjoyment and information, a child is taught.

When parents read to a child, a child is taught, and feels loved.

Teaching in a family is not just mother-to-child. There is so much to be learned from each other and extended family. Family time together is worth sacrificing for. I recently read a newspaper article describing family night in a community in New Jersey. It said that when "this commuter village 20 miles from New York decided [their] jam-packed schedules left no time for families, the calendars came out. It took seven months of planning, but on Tuesday, the upscale community of stately homes and gilt-lettered shops will take a collective night off."[2]

Other communities are doing the same thing. They are coming to understand what a prophet of God foresaw nearly a century ago when he called upon members of the Church to hold weekly family home evening. Children and parents need each other. They need planned teaching moments certainly, and they also need just plain old time—time when you work together, play together, laugh together—your time!

Journalist Dick Feagler suggests that "the trouble with the [quality time] notion is that being a kid is not a profession. Kids are not colleagues. . . . They lack the brisk efficiency to schedule quality time seminars with their parents. What kids do is hang out. And while they're hanging out, they want to know a parent is available. Not available to drive them to soccer practice or computer camp or gymnastics or baton-twirling. Just hanging out, too, somewhere around the house."[3]

Setting aside a weekly family night is a wonderful beginning. But I would say that it is only a minimal requirement for building a strong family foundation. I don't understand how you can build a firm, strong family foundation on one night a week. For many families the daily mealtime is a must.

Kitchens are an important place for teaching and adding building blocks to a family foundation. Mothers have no idea of the impact of their daily kitchen consistencies in nurturing their children.

What is so nice about mealtime is that food and prayers go together like salt and pepper or butter and jam. Whenever we got to eat breakfast at my grandparents' home, I noticed that grandma, who raised a large family, set the breakfast table the night before with the chairs turned away from the table. In the morning, before eating, we first knelt at our chairs to offer family prayer. "A generation or two ago," said President Gordon B. Hinckley, "family prayer in the homes of Christian people throughout the world was as much a part of the day's activity as were the meals. As that practice has diminished, our moral decay has ensued. I fear that as the quality of our housing has improved, the spirit of our homes has deteriorated."[4]

Isn't it ironic that in a day when the threats of evil in our society are so rampant, we are abandoning the very things that could strengthen and fortify us against evil?

In our family, six o'clock was a special hour in our home. Even though the boys were outside playing or working out with teams, or had jobs, or were in student government, everyone knew that at six o'clock there would be dinner waiting—table set, food ready. Those who were late without excuse got to do all the dishes. Otherwise, everyone pitched in and we could slick up the kitchen in short order and it was almost fun. Of course there were exceptions, but usually we all gathered at supper time to pray, share experiences of the day, tell the latest joke, coordinate schedules, discuss sports and current events and, on Sundays, the messages of the lessons and the speakers at church. For many families this is an ideal time to teach and add to the firm foundation of family.

Wise mothers have some vision of what they want their families to become. Teach your children about your vision for the family. When we were apartment dwellers, we would occasionally take Sunday drives through lovely neighborhoods with fine, large homes. I remember wondering, "If we could see the spiritual stature of that home out on the front lawn, would it tower over the house or barely fill one little corner of the lot?" And then, the time came when, with five growing children, we took on the project of building a new home. As the work progressed the home began to look larger than we had imagined and had the potential of seeming too wonderful. I worried about where we were placing our values as more and more time and resources were being consumed by this project. Finally one day we gathered our growing flock around us and said, "It would be sad if people drove by our house and said, 'Oh look at that beautiful home.' What I would hope is that people would drive by and say, 'Oh, the nicest family of outstanding children live in that home.' This home is where I want our children to come for love and security—a house wherein they learn the lessons of life and practice living the gospel." I guess this was really describing the blueprints of a house of God as outlined in the Doctrine and Covenants 88:119: "Establish a house, even a house of prayer, a house of fasting, a house of faith, a house of learning, a house of glory, a house of order, a house of God."

A vision of what your family can become and what that will require from you is a must in establishing a firm foundation to build upon.

Sometimes the vision has to be altered because part of your dream has been destroyed. Don't let a tragic happening destroy your foundation! It may feel shaky for a while, sometimes even a very long while, but if your faith is built on the solid ground of gospel teachings, on the rock of Christ, you can eventually steady your family once again. Look for ways to shore up the footings of faith—faith in the Lord Jesus Christ. He is the foundation upon which our lives must be built. It is He who implemented the Father's plan, and it is this plan you voted for. It is the great plan of happiness, a plan for success in meeting life's trials. Alma 7 teaches this: "And he shall go forth, suffering pains and afflictions and temptations of every kind; and this that the word might be fulfilled which saith he will take upon him the pains and the sicknesses of his people. And he will take upon him death, that he may loose the bands of death which bind his people; and he will take upon him their infirmities, that his bowels may be filled with mercy, according to the flesh, that he may know according to the flesh how to succor his people according to their infirmities" (vv. 11–12). Our beloved Savior provides succor for sickness, disappointment, tragedy, and adversity. He will carry those burdens for you. Ask for His help. He will help you. It is His work and His glory "to bring to pass the immortality and eternal life of man" (Moses 1:39). It is His mission to help you be successful in things of eternal worth. Seek His divine help. Turn to Him for rest from carrying your heavy burdens. Let faith in Him be the basis for your family foundation.

Always remember that "the most important of the Lord's work you will ever do will be within the walls of your own home."[5]

This means the greatest service you will ever give, the greatest lessons you will ever teach, the greatest leadership you will ever provide, the greatest music you will ever make will be those that strengthen the foundation of your home and bring your loved ones closer to the Savior.

Like the temple's firm foundation, once the family foundation is firmed up and the strength of the family is established, it can be there for eternity. It can endure forever. Such is our faith—even when you have a child who does not accept your teachings or example. Orson F. Whitney said, "The Prophet Joseph Smith declared— and he never taught more comforting doctrine—that the eternal sealings of faithful parents and the divine promises made to them for valiant service in the Cause of Truth, would save not only themselves, but likewise their posterity. Though some of the sheep may wander, the eye of the Shepherd is upon them, and sooner or later they will feel the tentacles of Divine Providence reaching out after them and drawing them back to the fold."[6]

This gives a brightness of great hope. This is a sweet promise. It is worth every effort. It is worth our finest efforts. It is worth our constant, enduring efforts.

"How firm a foundation, ye Saints of the Lord, is laid for your faith in his excellent word!"[7] May this be the song of your heart as you work with our Father in Heaven to build a firm, faithful foundation for your family. God will guide your hands and your mind as you build and strengthen your home and family. In this I have complete faith and testify of His goodness to His children as the master architect and the rock upon which we must build a firm foundation.

3

The Desire of Your Heart

A s you think about your children for whom you have so much love and concern, I have three questions for you to consider. They are serious questions and they are important. Please give them the greatest consideration as you contemplate your answers. (1) *What is the desire of your heart for your children?* Think about it very carefully. What is it that would bless their lives the very most? What could you give to them that they would cherish and love forever? While you consider the first question, let me ask a second: (2) *What does our Heavenly Father most desire for each of His children?* Now, before you answer too quickly, let me ask a third question: (3) *What does it mean to come unto Christ?*

I hope that thinking about these questions will lead you to determine that surely one of the most important things we can do for children is to help them love the Lord and want to draw close to Him. Isn't this most important—even more than popularity, good grades, sports, music, and dates? The work and the glory of the Lord is to bring to pass the "immortality and eternal life of man," and as members of the Church, we know of the importance of coming unto Christ. Then surely we must help our children love Him. I believe that it is just that simple. We must help them love Him, feel tender toward Him, be grateful for Him, know Him, honor Him, serve Him. When they really love Him, they will love His church and all that it stands for and teaches and requires. They will begin developing a firm foundation of faith planted deep in their hearts upon which they will build all the days of their lives.

Teach Your Children That They Are Sons and Daughters of God

Your first step in this process is to teach them that they really are spirit children of God, our Eternal Heavenly Father, and that our Savior, the Lord Jesus Christ, is His Son. We can help them know that Christ was sent by God our Father to show them the way to return home to Him. We can help them understand that He set the example for us to follow, that He sacrificed His very life, which was perfect in every way, to make it possible for them to come home again. He did this for them because He loves them so completely.

In some finite sense we may be able to help them understand about returning home from our mortal point of view. Elder Jeffrey R. Holland wrote about it:

> I recall . . . seeing a drama enacted at the Salt Lake airport. On this particular day, as I got off an airplane and walked into the terminal, it was immediately obvious that a missionary was coming home because the whole airport was astir with conspicuous-looking missionary friends and missionary relatives.
>
> I tried to pick out the immediate family members. There was a father who did not look particularly comfortable in an awkward-fitting and slightly out-of-fashion suit. He seemed to be a man of the soil, with a suntan and large, work-scarred hands. His white shirt was a little frayed and was probably never worn except on Sunday.
>
> There was a mother who was quite thin, looking as if she had worked very hard in her life. She had in her hand a handkerchief—and I think it must have

been a linen handkerchief once but now it looked like tissue. It was absolutely shredded from the anticipation only the mother of a returning missionary could know.

There was a beautiful girl who—well, you know about girls and returning missionaries. She appeared to be on the verge of cardiac arrest. I thought that if the young man didn't come soon, she would not make it without some oxygen.

Two or three younger brothers and sisters were running around, largely oblivious to the scene that was unfolding.

I walked past them all and started for the front of the terminal. Then I thought to myself, "This is one of the special human dramas in our lives. Stick around and enjoy it." So I stopped. I slipped into the back of the crowd to wait and watch. The passengers were starting to come off the plane.

I found myself starting to guess as to who would make the break first. I thought probably the girlfriend would want to most of all, but undoubtedly she was struggling with discretion. Two years is a long time, you know, and maybe one shouldn't appear too assertive. Then a look at that handkerchief convinced me that the mother was probably the one. She obviously needed to hold something, so the child she had carried and nurtured and gone down into the valley of the shadow of death to deliver would be just what the doctor ordered. Or perhaps it would be the boisterous little brother—if he happened to look up long enough to know the plane was in.

As I sat there weighing these options, I saw the missionary start to come down the stairs. I knew he was the one by the squeal of the crowd. He looked like Captain Moroni, clean and handsome and straight. Undoubtedly he had known the sacrifice this mission had meant to his father and mother, and it had made him exactly the missionary he appeared to be. He had his hair trimmed for the trip home, his suit was worn but clean, his slightly tattered raincoat was still protecting him from the chill his mother had so often warned him about.

He came to the bottom of the steps and started out across the apron toward our building and then, sure enough, somebody couldn't take it any longer. It wasn't the mother, and it wasn't the girlfriend, and it wasn't the rowdy little brother. That big, slightly awkward, quiet and bronzed giant of a man put an elbow into the ribcage of a flight attendant and ran, just simply ran, out onto that apron and swept his son into his arms.

The oxygen summoned for the girlfriend could have now been better directed toward the missionary. This big bear of a father grabbed him, took him clear off his feet, and held him for the longest time. He just held him and said nothing. The boy dropped his bag, put both arms around his dad, and they held each other very tightly. It seemed like all eternity stood still, and for a precious moment the Salt Lake City airport was the center of the entire universe. It was as if all the world had gone silent out of respect for such a sacred moment.[1]

And the child returned home. We are all our Father's children, and oh, how He wants us to come home again. What a remarkable trust He has placed in you to help His sons and daughters along their path back to Him! This is your calling, your duty given to you from God. The day that tiny newborn baby was placed in your arms was the beginning of a covenant made between you and our Father in Heaven to help this precious child return home to Him. In all you do you can help your children know how much Heavenly Father loves them and wants them back home again after successfully fulfilling their earthly missions. Teach them to love Him. Teach them of His love for them.

Teach Your Children the Father's Plan

In all His love, our Father in Heaven has a plan to help each of His children return home to Him. That plan involves the sacrifice and atonement of His only Begotten Son. The second step you can take in teaching your children is to help them gain a vision of the Savior's love and an understanding of God's marvelous plan. It is true that "we love him, because he first loved us" (1 John 4:19), as John taught.

When a child understands what the Atonement is, she will begin to understand the love Heavenly Father and the Savior, Jesus Christ, have for her. Think of the Savior who was willing to suffer for us. Even if you had been the only person on this earth, He would have suffered and been crucified for you. President Hinckley helped us understand the Atonement better with this instructive story:

> Years ago there was a little one-room schoolhouse in the mountains of Virginia where the boys were so rough that no teacher had been able to handle them. A young, inexperienced teacher applied, and the old director scanned him and asked, "Young fellow, do you know that you are asking for

an awful beating? Every teacher that we have had here for years has had to take one."

"I will risk it," he replied.

The first day of school came, and the teacher appeared for duty. One big fellow named Tom whispered, "I won't need any help with this one. I can lick him myself."

The teacher said, "Good morning, boys, we have come to conduct school." They yelled and made fun at the top of their voices. "Now, I want a good school, but I confess that I do not know how unless you help me. Suppose we have a few rules. You tell me, and I will write them on the blackboard."

One fellow yelled, "No stealing!" Another yelled, "On time." Finally, ten rules appeared on the blackboard.

"Now," said the teacher, "a law is no good unless there is a penalty attached. What shall we do with one who breaks the rules?"

"Beat him across the back ten times without his coat on," came the response from the class.

"That is pretty severe, boys. Are you sure that you are ready to stand by it?" Another yelled, "I second the motion," and the teacher said, "All right, we will live by them! Class, come to order!"

In a day or so, "Big Tom" found that his lunch

had been stolen. The thief was located—a little hungry fellow, about ten years old. "We have found the thief and he must be punished according to your rule—ten stripes across the back. Jim, come up here!" the teacher said.

The little fellow, trembling, came up slowly with a big coat fastened up to his neck and pleaded, "Teacher, you can lick me as hard as you like, but please, don't take my coat off!"

"Take your coat off," the teacher said. "You helped make the rules!"

"Oh, teacher, don't make me!" He began to unbutton, and what did the teacher see? The boy had no shirt on, and removal of the coat revealed a bony little crippled body.

"How can I whip this child?" he thought. "But I must, I must do something if I am to keep this school." Everything was quiet as death.

"How come you aren't wearing a shirt, Jim?"

He replied, "My father died and my mother is very poor. I have only one shirt and she is washing it today, and I wore my brother's big coat to keep me warm."

The teacher, with rod in hand, hesitated. Just then "Big Tom" jumped to his feet and said,

"Teacher, if you don't object, I will take Jim's licking for him."

"Very well, there is a certain law that one can become a substitute for another. Are you all agreed?"

Off came Tom's coat, and after five strokes the rod broke! The teacher bowed his head in his hands and thought, "How can I finish this awful task?" Then he heard the class sobbing, and what did he see? Little Jim had reached up and caught Tom with both arms around his neck.

"Tom, I'm sorry that I stole your lunch, but I was awful hungry. Tom, I will love you till I die for taking my licking for me! Yes, I will love you forever!" (Adapted from a story by Rev. A. C. Dixon, in Stan and Sharon Miller and Sherm and Peggy Fugal, *Especially for Mormons*, 5 vols. [Provo, Utah: Kellirae Arts, 1971–87], 4:37–38.)

To lift a phrase from this simple story, Jesus, my Redeemer, has taken "my licking for me" and yours for you.[2]

You can help your children know this with a testimony that sinks deep down into their hearts. The beautiful thing is that this love didn't end at Gethsemane or on Calvary. His love is available to guide us and help us each day, with every step along the way. God promised us this when He said: "For behold, this is my work and my glory—to bring to pass the immortality and eternal life of man" (Moses 1:39).

You are an instrument in His hands. You have been called to help Him by virtue of motherhood. You can receive inspiration to meet the needs of your precious child. You know this and have had experience with it. I hope you remember those times and find strength and encouragement from them.

Teach Your Children by Example

Every day you can invite His Spirit into your home. You are the teachers there. There is no greater call in all the world than to be a teacher of your children. There is a wonderful scripture in Mosiah that applies to each of us who teaches: "And also trust no one to be your teacher nor your minister, except he be a man of God, walking in his ways and keeping his commandments" (Mosiah 23:14). This places a responsibility on us to be women of God. As we teach our children about the Atonement, about the Father's plan, and that they are sons and daughters of God, we must remember to always walk in His ways and we must keep His commandments. We have to live the kind of exemplary life that a child can trust. We must be an example they can follow. The third step in the teaching process is to recognize that your life is your strongest, most powerful message to your children. What you are teaches more than anything you could ever say. Paul taught this principle when he wrote: "Thou therefore which teachest another, teachest thou not thyself? thou that preachest a man should not steal, dost thou steal?" (Romans 2:21).

When you teach a child with the help of the Spirit and with your life as an example, the message will take root in her life. Doctrine and Covenants 42:14 states: "And the Spirit shall be given unto you by the prayer of faith; and if ye receive not the Spirit ye shall not teach." To me that is saying that you will be given the Spirit of the Lord if you seek for it with faith, and it is not hard at all to access that Spirit. But we are told that you will not be effective in your teaching without the Spirit of the Lord, for it truly is the Spirit that teaches. I also believe that this scripture is saying that unless we have sought for the Spirit of the Lord to guide us then we probably shouldn't try to teach. I know with Nephi that when you "ask, . . . it shall be given unto you; seek, and ye shall find; knock, and it shall be opened unto you" (3 Nephi 14:7).

You will be blessed and guided from on high as the Holy Ghost whispers impressions to your heart and mind. Seek for this inspiration, listen for it, and then act on it.

A Desire to Come unto Christ

Let us return to where we began: *What is the desire of your heart for your children? What does our Heavenly Father most desire for each of His children—including you?* He asks that we love Him. Simply love Him. Come unto Christ. We draw close to Him as we pray and study the scriptures and live principled lives of integrity. We show by our actions, by our words, and by our lives that we truly do love Him. We can bear our testimony often by our words. We can bear our testimony *always* by our actions. We are taught so well by Matthew: "Wherefore by their fruits ye shall know them" (Matthew 7:20).

May we all be blessed to come unto Christ so that one day we can be embraced in the arms of His holy love. The late apostle Melvin J. Ballard, grandfather of Elder M. Russell Ballard, helps us catch a small glimpse of what this might feel like. He shared the following experience in the testimony that he bore to the First

Presidency and the Council of the Twelve in 1919, the day he was ordained an Apostle:

> Two years ago, about this time, I had been on the Fort Peck Reservation for several days with the brethren, solving the problems connected with our work among the Lamanites. Many questions arose that we had to settle. There was no precedent for us to follow, and we just had to go to the Lord and tell Him our troubles, and get inspiration and help from Him. On this occasion I had sought the Lord, . . . and that night I received a wonderful manifestation and impression which has never left me. . . . I saw myself here with you. I was told there was another privilege that was to be mine; and I was led into a room where I was informed I was to meet someone. As I entered the room I saw, seated on a raised platform, the most glorious being I have ever conceived of, and was taken forward to be introduced to Him. As I approached He smiled, called my name, and stretched out His hands toward me. If I live to be a million years old I shall never forget that smile. He put His arms around me and kissed me, as He took me into His bosom, and He blessed me until my whole being was thrilled. As He finished I fell at His feet, and there saw the marks of the nails; and as I

kissed them, with deep joy swelling through my whole being, I felt that I was in heaven indeed. The feeling that came to my heart then was: Oh! if I could live worthy, though it would require fourscore years, so that in the end when I have finished I could go into His presence and receive the feeling that I then had in His presence, I would give everything that I am or ever hope to be![3]

4

That Our Children May Know to What Source They May Look

There are many issues that our children face in today's world. Among them are gender roles; preparation for future responsibilities; moral purity; peer pressure; modesty in behavior, in speech, and in appearance; and staying close to family and the Church. Our children can be strengthened as we help them know to what source they may look to find encouragement and strength as they face challenges in their lives. Here I would like to focus on four important sources to which our children may look: doctrine and principles, parents, leaders, and the Lord.

Look to Doctrine and Principles

Our children can find strength and safety in doctrine and true principles. Elder Boyd K. Packer has taught that "true doctrine, understood, changes attitudes and behaviors."[1]

We know that our children were once mature spirits. We must remember that they have been taught by God Himself—and not that long ago. They don't need any more fluff in their lives. They are immersed in plenty of that by virtue of living in the world. What they need is a better understanding of gospel truths. What President J. Reuben Clark said many years ago is still true today: "[They] are hungry for the things of the spirit; they are eager to learn the Gospel, and they want it straight, undiluted. . . .

". . . You do not have to sneak up behind [them] and whisper religion in [their] ears. . . . You can bring these truths [out] openly."[2]

A clear understanding of gospel principles has great power. My friend Silvia Allred was fifteen when she joined the Church in El Salvador with her seventeen-year-old sister. At the time, they were the only members in their family. Today Silvia is a grandmother. She has served with her husband as he presided over a mission and has been a member of the Young Women general board. Her numerous posterity are all faithful members of the Church. I asked her what kept her true and faithful when she was so alone as a teenager. She said it was her deep conviction of the divinity of the Savior, her testimony of the power of the Atonement, and her commitment to obey the commandments. I think that is so remarkable. It was her testimony that served her so well in the teenage years and beyond.

We have so much that is wonderful to teach, and that which we teach must be more powerful and more satisfying than what the world offers.

Most children want to be successful. They want to be respected, to have influence, and to amount to something. In an age of situational ethics, microwave pushbuttons, and instant everything—with magazines and books touting quick fixes to every problem—it is easy to see how children could be confused about life's best processes. Children need to be taught to look to doctrine and principles for strength, power, safety, and enduring value.

In a *Deseret News* editorial, Jay Evensen cited a 1998 review by Duke and Vanderbilt Universities of forty separate studies on the relationship between religion and crimes committed by young people. The majority of these studies, Evensen wrote, "demonstrated a strong relationship between religious worship and low levels of delinquency. They also found that many people who commit crimes or become drug addicts report that they stopped going to church when they became adolescents. Studies show religious people have lower crime rates, lower levels of sexual promiscuity, better health and a better chance of escaping poverty and despair than people who don't actively believe in a God. Yet, other studies have found that social scientists tend to discount this relationship [between religiosity and levels of delinquency]."[3]

In Helaman 5:4 we learn that "it came to pass that Nephi had become weary because of [the people's] iniquity; and he yielded up the judgment-seat, and took it upon him to preach the word of God all the remainder of his days, and his brother Lehi also, all the remainder of his days." Here is a very important pedagogical concept at work: Perhaps the most effective way to change behavior is to teach *doctrine,* from which emerge *principles,* which, when understood, lead to *behavior.*

Elder Packer explains that "the study of the doctrines of the gospel will improve behavior quicker than a study of behavior will improve behavior."[4] Parents and sometimes leaders, usually out of frustration, spend time and energy chiding, hectoring, and railing on the behavior of their children. When they transfer their attention to the principles and doctrines of the gospel, they obtain better long-term results (not to mention lower blood pressure).

In summary, the first point is that our children's lives will be blessed if they learn to look to the doctrine and principles of the Church as the source of their strength and success in life.

Look to Parents

A second place children may look to is parents. A little story illustrates this point. One evening a family was sitting around the family room, the little children playing at the feet of their parents, when the three-year-old boy, out of the blue, said, "3 Nephi, chapter 11, verse 33." Somewhat startled, the father perked up and asked, "What did you say, Son?" The little boy repeated the scripture reference. The parents looked at each other quizzically and then decided he must have learned it in Primary. The mother opened her Book of Mormon to see what this child might be talking about and recognized this scripture about baptism: "And whoso believeth in me, and is baptized, the same shall be saved; and they are they who shall inherit the kingdom of God."

The parents might have left it at that or left it to the Primary to teach their child the doctrine of baptism. But they understood the instruction given by the Lord: "And again, inasmuch as parents have children in Zion, or in any of her stakes which are organized, that teach them not to understand the doctrine of repentance, faith in Christ the Son of the living God, and of baptism and the gift of the Holy Ghost by the laying on of the hands, when eight years old, the sin be upon the heads of the parents" (D&C 68:25).

The responsibility belongs to the parents to teach the doctrines and principles of the gospel. These parents nourished the seed planted in a Sunbeam class, and the whole family memorized and discussed 3 Nephi 11:33 and other scriptures after that.

Another day when this mother looked for her little boy, she found him sitting on the bottom stair with the Book of Mormon open in his lap, albeit upside down. He told her he loved the scriptures. And he was reading them like Mommy and Daddy do. This young family had already established a foundation upon which to build testimony in their children.

I remember sitting with our family to read scriptures, each boy taking his turn. My very favorite part was when the newest reader was called on. One day we were in the Beatitudes. And our little first grader was the newest reader. He tried to sound out each word with lots of help. He read, haltingly, "Blessed are the merciful for they shall . . ." and then without any help at all he blurted out, "orbit Mercury!" We couldn't help it; we all burst into laughter. And he joined us as we hugged and cheered his efforts. Surely to his young, imaginative eyes, "obtain mercy" looked like "orbit Mercury."

Years later, when he studied this scripture as a missionary, I hope that for a fleeting moment his memory went back to the happy day he and his family read the Beatitudes together.

It's not always easy to get children in a mood to join the family in scripture reading. Remember to keep it happy, keep it light. Serious times come soon enough.

Our family has tried every way we could think of: early morning on Mom and Dad's bed, or at supper with meatloaf and Moroni. Many times we read with friends joining in. We tried on Sundays, on Mondays, sometimes awake, sometimes not. Sometimes it took us a long time to finish one of the books because we discussed what we read, and sometimes our reading was short to match attention spans. In fact, we remember saying good-bye to a missionary son and promising him we'd try to finish the Book of Mormon as a family by the time he returned.

We weren't perfect in our scripture reading. We wanted to be and we tried lots of ways to be perfect in it, and we did the best we could under the circumstances.

Parents should be a child's first teacher of correct principles. But that is not all. I have chosen to highlight three other responsibilities. The first of these is the all-encompassing notion of *example*.

As a parent you teach the gospel through the way you live. Let your example of integrity and love for gospel living be one that youth can follow, one that they will want to follow.

Let your children feel safe as they look to your example. What a blessing when there is nothing amiss in the lives of parents, when language is kindly and intent is pure. Let us treat our children with respect. Let us endeavor to keep the harsh and the coarse out of our language.

What a blessing it would be to have a child say, "I

think of the examples of my parents in my parenting and in Church service. I'm grateful for their righteous lives, for their tireless devotion to gospel living, and I am grateful for their constant teaching and example of gospel principles."

As parents we can be examples of the positive effects of living with honesty and integrity in all we do. Even in the face of disappointment or betrayal by others—especially in those cases—we can look to gospel truths for hope. It is by holding to eternal truths that we can be an example of hope for a brighter future.

President Hinckley says his father used to tell him that "more religion is caught than is taught."[5] What we are doing as parents is contagious! We cannot afford to be indifferent or wavering or weak. We must speak with a strong voice for that which is right, and we must do it in happy and appealing ways!

Do your children know from your example and attitude that you value womanhood? Do your girls know that it is a privilege and a joy to be a woman, that it is a divine and priceless blessing from God? In a world where gender roles are questioned and even outdated in popular media, I believe in the teachings of God regarding our divine nature. Let your daughter know that she was feminine and female long before her physical body began to develop inside her mother. The spirit that gives life to her body is female. In other words, she is "all girl" from the inside out.

Likewise, the spirit that gives life to a boy's body is male. And he is "all boy." Prophets teach in the Proclamation on the Family that "gender is an essential characteristic of individual, premortal, mortal, and eternal identity and purpose."[6]

We must help our young men and our young women to value and honor the family above all else.

The Proclamation is so very clear about priorities for parents. Can we show our children that we are in tune with this teaching by our example? The Proclamation reads, "By divine design, fathers are to preside over their families in love and righteousness and are responsible to provide the necessities of life and protection for their families. Mothers are primarily responsible for the nurture of their children. In these sacred responsibilities, fathers and mothers are obligated to help one another as equal partners."[7]

What better compliment can be given a father than was expressed by a small boy when asked what he wanted to be when he grew up. His answer was, "Like my daddy." I know his daddy, and if he is like him it will bless his life forever. May it be the blessing of our children to find, in their parents, worthy examples.

Let us keep in mind what the German author and novelist Jean Paul Richter (1763–1852) once said: "What a father says to his children is not heard by the world, but it will be heard by posterity."

Now let us turn from example and consider the importance of work. Children need to look to their parents to be taught how to *work*. There is no substitute for learning how to work. It is one of the most important values that can be acquired in this life, and should be taught early and taught in the family. Children need to know that they are part of the family engine and not part of the baggage. Our ancestors whose lives were lived in largely rural environments learned that work was a natural part of everyday life. The pioneers would never have made it across the plains if the teenagers had ridden in the wagons.

Learning to work is a greater challenge in our modern society, but it is no less important to the success of our children. As our sons were growing up, my husband and I tried very hard to find work for them to do. They love to remind us that at times we were quite creative at it. They like to recall one Saturday morning when my husband and I were leaving to go on an assignment and they were imagining a whole Saturday of unsupervised free time. A huge dump truck drove up to our home and dumped an enormous load of dirt on our driveway and pulled away. Their version of that story is that their dad gathered all of them around the huge pile of dirt and said, "Boys, we need to raise the level of the back yard by six inches. Please have this dirt hauled out there and spread around by the time we get home."

How critical it is to learn to work. But it's also important to have *fun*.

As I was reading the minutes (which we kept occasionally) from our family home evenings during 1986, I noticed a definite pattern. We had a song and a prayer, paid allowances, praised each boy for something wonderful he had done (like a good spelling test or making his bed), and then we timed them while they ran to do forgotten chores. We had a short message, and then we went down to the local park and had a game of family soccer. Every week! We must have liked soccer. The boys could choose what would be fun and it was always the same. I'd love to know what a family of girls or a mixture of sons and daughters would choose.

We also had an old boat, which we bought and used with another family. One time we took it and the children (they were always happy to come boating) and went out into the middle of a nearby lake.

Steve turned off the engine and, as we floated there for a few minutes, no escape possible, we passed around the licorice and then he said, "You know boys, there is a little something I've been wanting to talk to you about." And then he taught them. But it was short. Short lessons were the key in our family of active boys.

You do what it takes to love, to teach, to have fun, to work, and to build unity in a family. But children must know to what source they may look . . . and parents are the scripturally mandated source!

"And ye will not suffer your children that they go hungry, or naked; neither will ye suffer that they transgress the laws of God, and fight and quarrel one with another, and serve the devil, who is the master of sin. . . . But ye will teach them to walk in the ways of truth and soberness; ye will teach them to love one another, and to serve one another" (Mosiah 4:14–15).

To summarize the second major point, children

need to know they can look to their parents to be teachers of true principles, to be steady examples of correct living, to teach the value of work, and to have fun.

Look to Leaders

Third, children need to look to their leaders. I watched a small child who was in attendance at the opening of a children's exhibit at the Museum of Church History and Art when along came President Howard W. Hunter in his wheelchair.

The prophet enjoyed the exhibit for a time and then began moving on. Just as he was leaving, the little boy looked up and recognized the President of the Church. As the boy turned and ran after President Hunter, we heard him say, "Follow the prophet, follow the prophet!" What a blessing for our children to be able to look to a living prophet as a source of guidance in these latter days.

President David O. McKay was the prophet of my youth. My, how we loved him! President Gordon B. Hinckley describes him as

> a tall and handsome man, physically robust, he loved the contest, his mind was scintillating and his wit delightful. His was a buoyant personality, he was

always encouraging, lifting up, seeing the bright side of things, and challenging others to move forward.

On one occasion he submitted to a lengthy interview from an internationally renowned writer who had interviewed the great and famous of the world. President McKay's secretary told me that when this man came out of the President's office after a long question and answer session, he said to her, "Today, for the first time in my life, I have talked with a prophet. I have spoken with a most remarkable man, who will stand out always in my mind as one who is preeminent among the many with whom I have spoken over the years and across the world. I have had an unusual and wonderful experience for which I am grateful."[8]

There are highlights that stand apart in a life as significant. One such moment in my life was a personal meeting with President McKay when I was in college. What a thrill it was when I received an invitation to meet with the President of the Church, along with a group of other young people!

I remember my great feelings of unpreparedness for such an interview, but I also remember thinking how marvelous it would be if I could sit close to him and receive his personal counsel to me.

I was determined to be spiritually prepared for this special visit. With a prayer in my heart, I read my scriptures all the way from Provo to Salt Lake City. Yes, it was typical of the "cramming" style of a college student, but it must have worked because the meeting was wonderful. As we arrived at President McKay's apartment at the Hotel Utah, several of the apostles were leaving and they stopped to greet us. Then I met the prophet.

He invited us to sit with him on the couch and he took my youthful hand in his large, warm prophet's hand for the duration of the meeting. I will forever remember the great warmth and love I felt in his presence as he talked with us.

All too soon the visit ended and I realized that there had been no personal advice for any of us. In fact, the words of the meeting have left my memory, but priorities became very clear that day. I had heard the prophet teach principles from the pulpit many times, and on this day I understood in a very personal way that when the prophet speaks he is speaking to me—and to you. Ever since then I have listened carefully when the prophet speaks because I know his words give sure guidance for our lives.

It is such a great blessing for our children to be able

to look to a living prophet as a source of guidance in these latter days. Members of the Church sustain wholeheartedly the First Presidency and Quorum of the Twelve Apostles as prophets, seers, and revelators. We love to follow their counsel for we know that in so doing there is safety and peace.

The First Presidency speaks directly to our children in the wonderful booklet *For the Strength of Youth.* Each sentence is powerful. I would like to share just some of their words:

> We promise that as you keep these standards and live by the truths in the scriptures, you will be able to do your life's work with greater wisdom and skill and bear trials with greater courage. You will have the help of the Holy Ghost. You will feel good about yourself and will be a positive influence in the lives of others. You will be worthy to go to the temple and to receive holy ordinances. These blessings and many more can be yours.
>
> We pray for each of you. May you keep your minds and bodies clean from the sins of the world so you can do the great work that lies before you. We pray that you will be worthy to carry on the responsibilities of building the kingdom of God and preparing the world for the Second Coming of the Savior.[9]

Surely our children will be blessed if they will learn to look to the prophet as their leader.

There is something else that can be learned as children look to their leaders as well as their parents. The greatest blessing these adults can give to young people is a vision of who they are and what they can become.

It is not by accident that young women worldwide are encouraged to stand each Sunday to recite the Young Women theme, which begins, "We are daughters of our Heavenly Father who loves us and we love Him." Each week young women are reminded of who they are and of the relationship they have with their Heavenly Father.

The statement of Aaronic Priesthood Purposes provides a similarly strong vision to young men so that they too know clearly who they are and what is expected of them.

My husband, Stephen, wrote about an experience he had with a group of young men:

> It was Sunday morning, and there, about twenty-five feet up in the top of the very large tree in our front yard, was a big, strong, eighteen-year-old boy. He was wearing his Sunday clothes—white shirt, tie, nice pants. He was surrounded on nearby

limbs by six or seven others in similar attire. Their most prominent features were the big grins they had on their faces. I have no idea what our nonmember neighbor friends thought. I suppose it looked like a flock of very strange birds had swooped out of the sky and landed in our tree. They were having just as much fun taking the fifteen rolls of toilet paper out of the tree as they undoubtedly had putting it in the trees the Saturday night before.

This was not our first experience with that particular flock of priests. I had been the Young Men president and their quorum advisor for several years and had come to know them as an energetic, playful, and an altogether typical group of sixteen- to eighteen-year-old boys. Indeed, as I looked at the boy highest in the tree, I remembered a remark I had made to Margaret several years earlier—something about why didn't this boy's parents do a little better job with him? Of course, our own boys were then three and four years old, so we were in the best possible position to render an expert opinion on these matters. Now that Margaret and I had seven teenage sons of our own, you can only imagine how many times I have eaten those words.

In 1997, nearly twenty-five years later, we saw that flock of priests again. One of them organized a reunion for us all at general conference time. There was the former bishop and his wife, Margaret and I, and eighteen of the nicest Melchizedek Priesthood holders you have ever seen! They came from California, Oregon, Washington, Idaho, and Louisiana. They were Scoutmasters, bishops, and elders quorum presidents, fathers, and husbands. They loved the gospel and they loved the Lord, and oh, how they loved their families.

The boy highest in the tree? The ringleader? The one about whom I had said to Margaret: "I think he's a nice-looking boy, honey, but I think he's just a scatter-brained football player!" Yes, he was there. I knew he would be. Three years before, I had visited a stake conference in Louisiana with the assignment to reorganize the stake presidency. I had been told about a wonderful young counselor in the stake presidency who would have made a great stake president had he not just moved. He had been a professor at the university, had a national reputation in his field, and had been recruited by other universities around the country. I asked his name. I asked it again. "Naw, it couldn't be," but it was! That big bird, the football player, had his Ph.D., was a nationally renowned scientist, and had served in a stake presidency. Oh yes, he was there with his wife and family. I threw my arms around him and he hugged me so hard it about broke my back. Gratefully, some things never change![10]

What a joyous reunion we had! It was a grand celebration. We celebrated Aaronic Priesthood boys becoming Melchizedek Priesthood men. We celebrated a bishop who never gave up. We celebrated parents who really had taught correct principles. We celebrated Leo, who had driven all night from California and parked his eighteen-wheeler the full length of our residential lot. Stephen says of that occasion,

I don't know how they did it. I didn't help them. But that Saturday night as I sat on the stand in the tabernacle looking out, there they all were, seated on the front row. I wondered where those ingenious boys had gotten tickets! What a special sight! Who could have imagined that that group of boys would one day all be seated together on the front row of the tabernacle for a general priesthood meeting. That weekend we laughed together, we embraced, we cried, we hugged, we talked, we ate together, and prayed together.

The morning after they left we awoke still basking in the glow of such an experience. We walked out on our front porch and there on our little new trees that could hardly hold leaves, we saw that each had been delicately and loving adorned with one carefully placed strand of white toilet paper.[11]

From that experience and others like it, we have learned how important it is for leaders and parents to believe in our youth and to share with them a vision of who they really are and the great contribution they can make as they become the future leaders of the Church.

Look to the Lord

The most important source to which our children and each of us may look is made clear in the complete verse from which the title of this chapter is taken. It reads as follows:

"And we talk of Christ, we rejoice in Christ, we preach of Christ, we prophesy of Christ, and we write according to our prophecies, that our children may know to what source they may look for a remission of their sins" (2 Nephi 25:26).

The ultimate success for our children as well as a measure of our success as parents will depend on how well we teach them to look to the Lord. Nephi clearly understood this important instruction. That is why he repeated for emphasis, "We talk of Christ, we rejoice in Christ, we preach of Christ, we prophesy of Christ."

Teaching children to look to the Lord ought to be foremost as we consider what and how to teach our children. This concept is effectively illustrated by a study of Latter-day Saint young men done some years ago by the Church Evaluation Division. The study analyzed the behavior of young men in the Church—their attendance at meetings, their participation in priesthood assignments, their relationship with advisers, and so on. The conclusions of the study were extended to young women and are reaffirmed, in general, in subsequent work completed by Brigham Young University professors Brent Top and Bruce Chadwick.[12]

The results are quite revealing. It turns out that the best predictor of missionary service for young men and temple marriage for young women and young men is *private religious observance*. It is not attendance at meetings. It is not participation in girls' camp or super activities or stake athletic programs. Those things are important, but only if they bring the Spirit and strengthen testimonies. The number one predictor is private religious observance or, in other words, looking to the Lord on an individual basis. Private religious observance is what goes on in the home—personal prayer, family prayer, scripture reading, tithe paying, and Sabbath day observance.

It is in these simple, private religious activities that our children really come to know the Lord, to know of His goodness and His mercy and love.

The object of our children's religious experience ought to be to learn to love the Lord. That is why it is so important that our zeal for teaching and training and requiring of our children not make them resentful of the Church because of our awkwardness or heavy-handedness.

In his teenage years, my husband was once taught well and helped ever so subtly to love and not resent the Lord and His commandments. He and a friend, Richard Sharp, were shooting hoops on the driveway of Richard's home one beautiful Sunday afternoon in Idaho Falls. Eventually, President John Sharp, Richard's father, drove up to the house, coming home from a meeting of the stake presidency. He leaned against the car and watched the boys playing. They eagerly coaxed him to come shoot a few baskets with them. His reply was simply, "Well, I don't think so boys, I guess I'll just watch you today." That was all. He didn't berate them

Margaret D. Nadauld

for not properly honoring the Sabbath day. He didn't shame them for not setting a good example as the son of a member of the stake presidency. He didn't scold them for knowing better than they were behaving.

He didn't belittle the neighbor boy for leading his son astray on the driveway with a basketball or any of the many other things he could have said. He just loved them both. They knew it and felt it as he stood there and just watched and taught by his example. They felt no resentment. They did feel loved and understood.

In time these very good boys came to understand what the example of that good and kind man had taught them. And they followed it. A few years later each boy served a mission, and it wasn't many years later that each became a bishop at a very young age— always with love for the Lord and His commandments foremost in their hearts, never with feelings of resentment.

Our lives are blessed in a magnificent way by the life and mission of our beloved Redeemer and Savior, the Lord Jesus Christ. I think it truly remarkable that the world still remembers that little baby boy born in Bethlehem so long ago. He grew from boy to man.

"And Jesus increased in wisdom and stature, and in favour with God and man" (Luke 2:52).

He lived a life that we still try to follow. He showed us the way. He performed miracles. He taught by parables. He taught truths we still try to live after two millennia, and the truths He taught are the truths of heaven. They are as true today as they were then.

He willingly suffered for our sins because He loved us so completely. Through His Atonement He gave us the right to repent. And He gave His life that we might be resurrected and live again after death. When our children know this for themselves they will know the true Source to which they may look all the days of their lives.

5
Fathers

I n this book for mothers I would like to include some words about fathers. The stripling warriors, who are so famous for following the faith of their mothers, were also blessed by their fathers. Helaman tells Captain Moroni not only about the influence of the mothers on these awesome boys but also about the fathers providing for their children (see Alma 56:27). These young men couldn't have been as successful without the provisions brought by faithful fathers. Do we give credit to and show appreciation for all that fathers do for families?

Recently my wonderful father passed away. He was the beloved patriarch of his family and of his stake. He had spent his lifetime in the service of his family and others. In reflecting on the life and goodness of this noble man, I have remembered some of the Christmases we had as children. As I was growing up, my father worked hard and provided well for our family. Every year Christmas morning was the same for us. We got up early—too early—awakened our parents, and joined together in the living room as we opened our gifts with unbridled enthusiasm, throwing the wrappings about, exclaiming with delight our joy in all we had received. And then, busily (and I must say in retrospect, selfishly), set about playing with and enjoying the abundance our parents had provided. Daddy slipped quietly out and went to the hatchery to do the work that had to be done. Thousands of eggs in incubators, in process of hatching into thousands of baby chicks, had to be carefully attended to and the parent stock fed and cared for. Daddy's employees had Christmas day off to be with their families, but chickens never have a day off. The work still had to be done, so our good-hearted father did it. In our youthful lack of understanding and appreciation, we were disappointed to have him leave so soon. Didn't he care about us? Did he love to work more than he loved to be with us?

And then one day I understood and I felt ashamed.

Daddy loved us more than anything; that is why he worked so hard to provide for us without ever, ever one word of complaint. I wonder if he ever felt unappreciated or unloved by his thoughtless daughter. We eventually outgrew and overcame that kind of behavior with the help of our wise mother.

"The Family: A Proclamation to the World" teaches that fathers "are responsible to provide the necessities of life and protection for their families."[1] Wives can show gratitude for all that their husbands do to provide for the family. They can express this gratitude within hearing of their children. When you go out for a hamburger with the family, do you make a point of saying thank you to your husband for doing dinner and dishes that night as he empties the fast food trays into the trash?

When you kneel in prayer as a couple and as a family, do you thank Heavenly Father for a husband who works hard? By example, a wise woman teaches her children to be grateful for all their father does. Her husband loves coming home because there he will find peace, refreshment, relief from the pressures of the world. He will find appreciation at home and there he will be loved.

You can help enhance the relationship between the children and their father. Daddies are so important to daughters in the establishment of self-image. Find ways to help fathers and children keep a close and happy relationship.

In a newspaper account of the most outstanding girls basketball player in the state, the young woman told a reporter, "'[My dad's] been my coach my whole life,' . . . 'He trains with me, runs with me, shoots with me. He helps me set my goals and has just always been there for me. He always wants the best for me.'"[2]

Our son James wrote the following for one of his application essays to Harvard: "Growing up, every Saturday morning was the same. My father wouldn't say anything; he would simply tap on our bedroom doors, then go outside. Within ten minutes his groggy sons, from teenager to toddler, would be at his side in our backyard. If there were in fact no pressing chores, we would simply move dirt. It was Saturday morning and we were working: that's what mattered to him. Eventually he would stop, wipe his brow and with a broad smile declare, 'It's a fine day for water-skiing.'

"After a couple of hours dragging us around the lake in an old boat we shared with another family, he'd stop in the middle of the water for lunch. Then, as we were all sitting there, his captive audience with bologna sandwiches in one hand and sodas in the other, my father would teach us. He taught us the value of hard work and priorities in the context of a well-balanced life. At the time I didn't know it. I was just enjoying my bologna sandwich, but it was during these moments that I learned many of the values I hold dear today."

Mothers, encourage involvement of fathers in the lives of your children and in the establishment of firm family foundations.

One of the first important occasions in the life of a child is the day he receives a name and a blessing from his father. One Sunday I was in attendance when a grateful young father gave his baby girl a name and a blessing. In the blessing she was told of her precious worth. Her father blessed her to be a girl who loves her Heavenly Father, a girl who will love the gospel, even sacrifice for it. He blessed her to be a light to others, to be kind, and to honor womanhood all the days of her life. He blessed her to be a true and faithful daughter of God so that one day she will be prepared to make and then live to keep sacred temple covenants. The sweet and tender desires of a parent's heart were expressed in that blessing.

Do you remember the blessings given to your children by their father? Have you told your children about them? Perhaps you have a record of them. You could review them and share them with your children. It will help them catch a vision of all their wonderful possibilities.

A mother is blessed by the faithful men in her life who hold the priesthood of God and honor this privilege: her husband, father, bishop, brothers, sons. They value her and the divine gifts given by God to His daughter. They sustain and encourage and understand the great mission of her life as a woman. They love her; they bless her. They are in turn blessed by this woman of faith as they walk the path of life together. They know, as scripture teaches, that "two *are* better than one, . . . For if they fall, the one will lift up his fellow" (Ecclesiastes 4:9–10; emphasis added).

How I love the great and good men who have lifted me up and encouraged me throughout my life. I am eternally grateful for the priesthood and the worthy men who bless my life and our children's lives with its holy power. May God bless honorable fathers. And may we in turn honor and bless their lives.

6

Of One Heart

When our twin sons were only about five years old they were just learning to ride their bicycles. As I glanced out the window, I saw them speeding down the street on their bikes going very fast! Perhaps they were going a little too fast for their level of ability because suddenly Adam had a terrible crash! He was so tangled up in the wreck that all I could see was a twist of handlebars and tires and arms and legs. His little twin brother, Aaron, saw the whole thing happen and immediately skidded to a stop and jumped off his bike. He threw it down and ran to the aid of his brother, whom he loved so much.

These little twins truly were of one heart. If one hurt, so did the other. If one got tickled, they both laughed. If one started a sentence, the other could finish it. What one felt, the other did also. So it was painful for Aaron to see Adam crash! Adam was a mess. He had skinned knees, he was bleeding from a head wound, his pride was damaged, and he was definitely crying. In a fairly gentle five-year-old way, Aaron helped his brother get untangled from the crash, he carefully checked out the wounds, and then he did the dearest thing. He picked his brother up and carried him home. Or tried to. This wasn't easy because they were the same size, but he tried.

As he struggled and lifted and half-dragged, half-carried his brother along, they finally reached the front porch. By this time, Adam, the injured one, was no longer crying, but Aaron, the rescuer, was. When I asked, "Why are you crying, Aaron?" He said simply, "Because Adam hurts."

He had brought him home to help, home to someone who knew what to do, to someone who could cleanse the wounds, bind them up, and make it better. Home to love. Home to mother. Mother, the heart of the home. Mother, who knows what to do. Mother, who can make it better.

It is through the love of a mother that children

learn what love is and how to give it in return. By her loving example, a mother makes it possible for her child to understand about our heavenly, eternal home and the role of our Heavenly Father and His Son, Jesus Christ.

What a blessing it is when your child comes to understand that she has a heavenly home as loving as the one she knows here on earth and that she is blessed with a brother who loves her and will lift her up and carry her with His perfect love to that home. Jesus Christ is so much more than our elder brother—He is our precious Savior, our dear Redeemer. He always knows what to do. He knows our hearts and wants us to know His.

What strength it is to our children when they understand that He wants us to be "of one heart" (Moses 7:18) with Him and our Father in Heaven. Just as one twin helped his brother in need, so might we all be lifted, helped, even carried at times by our beloved Savior, the Lord Jesus Christ. He feels what we feel; He knows our hearts. It is His mission to wipe away our tears, cleanse our wounds, and bless us with His healing power. He can carry us home to our Heavenly Father with the strength of His matchless love.

Surely He hears us when we cry in pain. He knows when we are going faster than we should. He will even be there for us if we are to make a wrong turn in disobedience to His teachings. I love the scripture that simply says, "Jesus wept" (John 11:35) when talking about the death of His dear friend, Lazarus.

Surely it pleases the Lord when we, His children—mothers, fathers, brothers, sisters—reach out in love to one another, to be His hands, to give help along the way, and to bring another closer to Christ. He taught, "[When] ye have done it unto one of the least of these my brethren, ye have done it unto me" (Matthew 25:40). He wants us to "mourn with those that mourn; yea, and comfort those that stand in need of comfort" (Mosiah 18:9) and "by love serve one another" (Galatians 5:13).

Mothers can help children come unto Christ, to be "of one heart" with our Father in Heaven and His Son.

We are reminded each week as we partake of the sacrament what it means to come unto Christ, to be of one heart with Him. We can teach our children about the importance of doing so. One way would be to help them show reverence for the sacred sacrament by keeping the Cheerios® and the books, markers and games put away until after the sacrament service. Children can learn at an early age about controlling themselves for at least that long. One young woman understood in her young years about the sacred nature of the sacrament service. She said that she likes partaking of the sacrament each week "because it reminds me of Jesus and all He did for me." Another said, "I never come away with an empty heart and I love taking the sacrament." Mothers can help their children feel a reverence for and a closeness to the Savior as they partake of the sacrament.

Another way mothers teach their children to come unto Him is through prayer. When asked how often they pray, many youth say "morning and night." What would your children answer? What about you? "Ere you left your room this morning, Did you think to pray?"[1] Have your children ever "caught" you praying as you sought heavenly help?

A stake president I know can remember kneeling at the railing in his crib as his mother stood there by him and taught him to pray.

I'm sure that prayer has been a source of strength to each of us at pivotal times. One such time happened for me when I was seven years old. I became seriously ill. Each day the illness became increasingly severe. Nothing the doctor recommended helped. At that time the dreaded disease of polio was raging in almost epidemic proportions in the land. It was taking the lives of many, and those who didn't die were often left crippled. Polio was everyone's worst fear in those days.

One night the illness became critical, and my father and grandfather administered to me using consecrated oil. Through the power of the holy Melchizedek Priesthood, which they held worthily, they called on God for healing, help, guidance, and comfort. And then my parents took me to a doctor in another town who immediately sent us to Salt Lake City—two-and-one-half hours away—with the admonition to hurry. I overheard the doctor whisper the word *polio*.

When we finally arrived at the hospital in Salt Lake, there were medical personnel waiting for us. They grabbed me from my parents' arms and whisked me away. Without a word of good-bye or explanation, we were separated. I was all alone, and I thought I was going to die.

After the painful diagnostic procedures, including a spinal tap, they took me to a hospital "isolation room," where I would stay all by myself with the hope that I would not infect anyone else, for indeed I had polio.

I remember how very frightened I was. It was dark and I was so sick and so alone. But my parents had taught me to pray. I got on my knees and knelt beside the railing in the criblike bed and asked Heavenly Father to bless me. I was crying, I remember. Heavenly Father heard my prayer even though I was only a child. He did. Heavenly Father sent His comforting power which enveloped me in quiet love. I felt the power of the Holy Ghost. I was not alone.

What a remarkable blessing it is to know about the mission of the Lord Jesus Christ. He loves us and He knows we need Him. He can help us and heal us. He understands us because of His own experiences. The scriptures report: "And he shall go forth, suffering pains and afflictions and temptations of every kind; . . . that he may know . . . how to succor his people according to their infirmities" (Alma 7:11–12).

We want to come unto Christ and help our children to do so because it is only in Him and through Him that we can return to the Father. Sometimes it is even our privilege to be sent on His errand and to be His arms to help lift and care for another.

Mothers have a remarkable influence for good on young hearts and souls as they teach their children of love, of renewing covenants at sacrament time, of prayer. By these means they, and we, can become of one heart with the keepers of our eternal home. May we each reach up to Him, feel of one heart with Him and find ourselves "encircled about eternally in the arms of his love" (2 Nephi 1:15).

7

The Light at the End of the Tunnel

~~~~~

S omeone recently said to me, "There is light at the end of the tunnel, . . . and it isn't an oncoming train!" That's a hopeful statement! But it made me remember tunnel times. I thought of Princess Diana's tragic ending in a tunnel in France, and I thought of the Chunnel built under the English Channel to connect England with France. I recalled all the tunnels I'd been in from Berkeley, California, to New Jersey and the tunnels on other continents as well. Tunnels always intimidate me a little.

When I was a child we had to go through a tunnel to get to our cousins' house on the other side of the mountain, a two-hour drive away. I was in awe of this huge hole drilled right through a mountain where inside they had built a two-lane road. To me, it was always an adventure to go through that tunnel and, frankly, it seemed a little scary. It was so dark in there! What a relief when we could catch the first glimpse of sunlight as we neared the end of the tunnel. With numerous trips in one side of the tunnel, through the mountain and out the other side, I came to know it wasn't dark for long and soon we would be in the light again. The funniest thing is, the older I got, the shorter the tunnel seemed to be and the less frightening it was. I came to have a sure knowledge of the outcome because of what experience had taught me.

Since childhood days, with all the many tunnels I have been through in different locations in this world, I have learned one very interesting thing: Without fail, there always, always was a light at the end of every one of those tunnels and never, ever was that light an oncoming freight train!

I believe that as it is with tunnels, so it is with mothering. Sometimes there are dark places in that journey but there is always light awaiting us just up ahead. There is even light we can tap into during the trip! That perfect light "groweth brighter and brighter until the perfect day" (D&C 50:24).

Three of the important elements that will make the light in our mothering brighter are the famous trio: faith, hope, and charity. Have you ever heard the old song that goes: "Have faith, hope, and charity. That's the way to live successfully. How do I know? The Bible tells me so"? The Savior, who is the light and life of the world, has invited us each to accept His invitation to come follow Him and to fear not but to have faith, to have hope, and to partake of His perfect charity.

How is your faith? Do you consider yourself a woman of faith? Could you see yourself walking two thousand miles across uncharted territory for your faith? Could you do that tomorrow? Do you have that kind of faith? Could you walk away from all you have and follow a prophet without a sure knowledge of where you were going to end up but willing to do all and give all anyway just because you had faith in God and in your leaders that there was a Zion awaiting you, that they would be led by God and that you could and should and must put your whole faith, even your very life in their hands and follow them?

Could you begin such a journey heavy with child?

Could you walk all those miles carrying a baby in your arms? Could you do it without a companion? And then, when everything went wrong and you were sick and tired and hungry, could you still believe in God? Mary Fielding Smith, the widow of Hyrum Smith, did and the record of her experiences is remarkable. We read that:

> Things went along quite smoothly until they reached a point midway between the Platte and the Sweetwater rivers, when one of Mary's best oxen lay down in the yoke as if poisoned and all supposed he would die. All the teams in the rear stopped, and many gathered around to see what had happened. In a short time, the Captain perceived that something was wrong and came to the spot. The ox stiffened in the throes of death. The Captain blustered about and exclaimed "He is dead, there is no use working with him, we'll have to fix up some way to take the Widow along. I told her she would be a burden on the company." But in this, he was greatly mistaken.
>
> Mary said nothing but went to her wagon and returned with a bottle of consecrated oil. She asked her brother Joseph and James Lawson to administer to her fallen ox, believing that the Lord would raise him. It was a solemn moment there under the open sky. A

hush fell over the scene. The men removed their hats. All bowed their heads as Joseph Fielding, who had been promised by Heber C. Kimball that he would have power to raise the dead, knelt, laid his hands on the head of the prostrate ox, and prayed over it. The great beast lay stretched out and very still. Its glassy eyes looked nowhere. A moment after the administration the animal stirred. Its huge, hind legs commenced to gather under it. Its haunches started to rise. The forelegs strengthened. The ox stood and, without urging, started off as if nothing had happened. This amazing thing greatly astonished the onlookers.

They hadn't gone very far when another ox, "Old Bully," lay down under exactly the same circumstances. This time it was one of her best oxen, the loss of which would have been very serious. Again, the holy ordinance was administered, with the same results.[1]

Mary Fielding Smith, the widow of Hyrum Smith, married him at age thirty-six and raised his five motherless children and two of her own. Her son is Joseph F. Smith, who became sixth president of the Church; her grandson Joseph Fielding Smith became the tenth president. She is the great-grandmother of M. Russell Ballard of the Quorum of the Twelve and of

Sister Sydney Smith Reynolds, first counselor in the Primary general presidency; the list of her righteous posterity goes on. It is estimated that today there are 35,000 descendants—the vast majority of whom are faithful members of the Church. The point is this: the faith of one good woman produced remarkable results.

Jane Allgood Bailey, a faithful Saint who traveled with the Martin Handcart Company, wasn't about to give up the light of her new religion. She would not be defeated by the cold, starvation, and sickness on the plains of Wyoming. She grasped hands with other women to wade through icy streams. They came out on the other side with their clothes frozen to them, but they carried on. On the trek, her eighteen-year-old son Langley became ill and was so weak that he had to be pushed on the handcart much of the way. One morning he rose from his bed on the cart, which had frozen canvas for bedding, and went ahead of the company and lay down under a sagebrush to die, feeling that he was too much of a burden. When his faithful mother found him, she scolded him and told him, "Get on the cart. I'll help you, but you're not giving up!" Then the family moved on with what was left of the ill-fated Martin Handcart Company. Upon arrival in the Salt Lake Valley, Langley was still alive! He was eighteen years old and weighed only sixty pounds. That eighteen-year-old boy was my great-grandfather.

President David O. McKay once related that members of a class were criticizing Church leaders for permitting the Martin Handcart Company to commence its journey so late in the season. He recalled that an old man of great faith listened to the criticism and then arose.

> In substance [he] said, "I ask you to stop this criticism. You are discussing a matter you know nothing about. Cold historic facts mean nothing here, for they give no proper interpretation of the questions involved. Mistake to send the Handcart Company out so late in the season? Yes. But I was in that company and my wife was in it and Sister Nellie Unthank whom you have cited was there, too. We suffered beyond anything you can imagine and many died of exposure and starvation, but did you ever hear a survivor of that company utter a word of criticism? Not one of that company ever apostatized or left the Church, because everyone of us came through with the absolute knowledge that God lives, for we became acquainted with him in our extremities.
>
> "I have pulled my handcart when I was so weak and weary from illness and lack of food that I could

hardly put one foot ahead of the other. I have looked ahead and seen a patch of sand or a hill slope and I have said, I can go only that far and there I must give up, for I cannot pull the load through it. . . . I have gone on to that sand and when I reached it, the cart began pushing me. I have looked back many times to see who was pushing my cart, but my eyes saw no one. I knew then that the angels of God were there.

"Was I sorry that I chose to come by handcart? No. Neither then nor any minute of my life since. The price we paid to become acquainted with God was a privilege to pay, and I am thankful that I was privileged to come in the Martin Handcart Company."[2]

Such faith is your heritage. You are a daughter of the same Father they had and you have the same stuff in you that they had.

The scriptures teach us about the faith we exhibited in our premortal life. Alma 13 explains about the faithful "being called and prepared from the foundation of the world according to the foreknowledge of God, on account of their exceeding faith and good works; in the first place being left to choose good or evil; therefore they having chosen good, and exercising exceedingly great faith, are called with a holy calling. . . . And thus they have been called to this holy calling on account of their faith, while others would reject the Spirit of God on account of the hardness of their hearts and blindness of their minds, while, if it had not been for this they might have had as great privilege as their brethren" (Alma 13:3–4).

We now find ourselves, because of the "exceedingly great faith" exhibited in our premortal life, in our mortal probation today. We have what we voted for! For us in mortality the veil is drawn and we must exhibit the same faith that led us to vote for our Heavenly Father's plan, which the Savior pledged to implement.

Do you have faith that the same God that parted the Red Sea, that guided Lehi and his family to the promised land, that led Brigham Young to the right place, is willing to also lead you to your promised land? To help you find light at the end of your tunnel? Of course He is. But is your faith sufficient? Are you willing to follow Him every step of the way, to hold the iron rod as you go, to seek His guidance and direction as you make your journey? Do you pray without ceasing? Do you read and know and understand His words as recorded in the scriptures and in the teachings of our latter-day prophets? Then you are a woman of faith and His light will be sufficient for you.

Elder Boyd K. Packer recorded a learning experience he had with faith:

> Some years ago I learned a lesson that I shall never forget.
>
> I had been called as an Assistant to the Council of the Twelve, and we were to move to Salt Lake City and find an adequate and permanent home. President Henry D. Moyle assigned someone to help us.
>
> A home was located that was ideally suited to our needs. Elder Harold B. Lee came and looked it over very carefully and then counseled, "By all means, you are to proceed."
>
> But there was no way we could proceed. I had just completed the course work on a doctor's degree and was writing the dissertation. With the support of my wife and our eight children, all of the resources we could gather over the years had been spent on education.
>
> By borrowing on our insurance, gathering every resource, we could barely get into the house, without sufficient left to even make the first monthly payment.

Brother Lee insisted, "Go ahead. I know it is right."

I was in deep turmoil because I had been counseled to do something I had never done before—to sign a contract without having the resources to meet the payments.

When Brother Lee sensed my feelings he sent me to President David O. McKay, who listened very carefully as I explained the circumstances.

He said, "You do this. It is the right thing." But he extended no resources to make the doing of it possible.

When I reported to Brother Lee he said, "That confirms what I have told you."

I was still not at peace, and then came the lesson. Elder Lee said, "Do you know what is wrong with you—you always want to see the end from the beginning."

I replied quietly that I wanted to see at least a few steps ahead. He answered by quoting from the sixth verse of the twelfth chapter of Ether: "Wherefore, dispute not because ye see not, for ye receive no witness until after the trial of your faith."

And then he added, "My boy, you must learn to walk to the edge of the light, and perhaps a few steps into the darkness, and you will find that the light will appear and move ahead of you."

And so it has—but only as we walked to the edge of the light.[3]

It is my testimony that God cares. He sent His Son to show us the way, and all we have to do is have the faith to follow Him. We can even reach out to Him and "[He will] lead [us] by the hand, and give [us] answer to [our] prayers" (D&C 112:10). When we do this, when we give our lives over to Him, the way is easier because we won't be making mistakes that bring us sorrow and pain. We will avoid self-inflicted pain. That should greatly cut down on this life's suffering. There is enough sorrow and trial that comes just from living in this world and being subject to the laws of nature and the agency of mankind.

Alma taught that the Savior promised to help us bear all of life's afflictions: "And he shall go forth, suffering pains and afflictions and temptations of every kind; and this that the word might be fulfilled which saith he will take upon him the pains and the sicknesses of his people" (Alma 7:11).

In addition to Christ's willingness to take upon Himself our pains, He also suffered for our sins. Should you make an avoidable mistake, or commit sin, and thus inflict pain into your life, He will even help you deal with that because He made repentance possible. What a blessed and divine and holy and hopeful principle! Those who partake of that great gift of the Lord Jesus Christ can be whole and happy and well once again. There will be no more "foreigners and strangers" feelings in you, no feelings of second-class citizenship in the Church; you can be like a new person. It will be as if you were cleansed once again in the waters of baptism.

What a very real process that is. Perhaps not quite as graphic as our eight-year-old son thought, though. On the day of his baptism, soon after his eighth birthday, we dressed him all in white and with great anticipation stood with him at the side of the baptismal font just prior to the beginning of the services for our ward. Another ward in the stake had just finished their baptismal services and now it was our turn. As Justen stood there and looked carefully into the water where soon he would be with his father, he spotted a few little dark specks floating on the surface of the water. He considered them for a moment and then looked up at me and in all earnestness asked, "Mom, see those black specks on the water?" "Yes," I replied. "Mom," he asked, "Are those sins?"

Don't you love knowing that each week, as you partake of the sacrament worthily, you have the remarkable privilege of once again renewing your baptismal promises? You have the opportunity of being cleansed, getting rid of those dark specks in your life, of repenting and going forward into the next week refreshed, recommitted, faithful. Such are the privileges of faith, faith in the Lord Jesus Christ and the repentance He made possible for us through the Atonement.

This week, would you assess your life, and if you find that your faith needs strengthening, would you begin immediately to take the steps to increase your faith? You know how. Follow Christ. Jesus said, "Come, follow me" (Luke 18:22). If in His footsteps we would tread, we must walk in His path.

To increase faith, pray with all your heart to your Father in Heaven, who loves you, always loves you. Study and ponder His words and keep His commandments so He can bless you. Do all in your power to increase your faith in the power and love of the Lord Jesus Christ for you personally.

As your faith grows and increases so will the light in

your life grow until you have "a perfect brightness of hope." Nephi taught: "Wherefore, ye must press forward with a steadfastness in Christ, having a perfect brightness of hope, and a love of God and of all men. Wherefore, if ye shall press forward, feasting upon the word of Christ, and endure to the end, behold, thus saith the Father: Ye shall have eternal life" (2 Nephi 31:20).

Do you take the 13th Article of Faith as part of your personal philosophy of life? Is it part of your creed, your motto, your guide? "We believe all things, *we hope all things,* we have endured many things, and hope to be able to endure all things" (Articles of Faith 1:13; emphasis added).

One of the most hopeful statements I've heard President Hinckley make is this: "It will work out." When a man who has seen ninety-plus years of living, who is also a prophet of God, says that, I take great hope! There is nothing more encouraging than hope.

An airline pilot tells of flying from the West Coast to Salt Lake International Airport at nighttime as part of his regular route. He reports that when he was over central Utah he always looked for the beautiful pioneer

Manti Temple, built on a hill and all lit up at night and shining out of the dark night sky, reaching up to him as a beacon of light. Even in a snowstorm he could see that brilliant light as it shone heavenward. When he saw the light of that temple, a feeling of hope settled over him, for seeing it showed him he was on the right course to reach his destination and that it wouldn't be much longer now.

In the storms of life you and I can find great hope for success as we follow the Savior—the light of His example will show us the way. The bright light of His love shines out as a beacon to us. It is hopeful to know that He has had experience and expertise in traveling this earth. He will show us the way. That is His mission. The Lord is our light and we can rely on His guidance to provide hope in our life's storms.

Do you have hope for the future? Do you live ready to partake of the blessings you hope for? Does your faith give you hope? Do your plans give you hope? What do you hope for? What are the deepest desires of your heart? What are you doing to make your hopes and dreams become reality? What is there in your life that would dim your hopeful attitude? Is there a "snowstorm," so to speak, in your life that makes your vision limited and that has you frightened and fearful? My testimony is that there is hope! And there is help just up ahead of you.

That help comes in the form of the third part of my formula for finding light at the end of life's tunnels: charity or, in other words, love.

As my father lay in the hospital in the last days of his life there were many sweet and tender words spoken and sacred experiences shared as the veil grew thinner and his spirit hovered between heaven and earth. I remember so well the times this great, good man said to us, "Let us have love for all mankind." At the end of a long life well lived, he was concerned about the importance of love filling the earth.

We can begin to fill the earth with love by first filling our own life with love, with charity. What are you doing on a daily basis to cultivate your capacity to love others; to love your children, your husband, your parents, your co-workers; to love yourself? We can learn about charity as we study 1 Corinthians:

> Though I speak with the tongues of men and of angels, and have not charity, I am become as sounding brass, or a tinkling cymbal.
>
> And though I have the gift of prophecy, and

understand all mysteries, and all knowledge; and though I have all faith, so that I could remove mountains, and have not charity, I am nothing.

And though I bestow all my goods to feed the poor, and though I give my body to be burned, and have not charity, it profiteth me nothing.

Charity suffereth long, and is kind; charity envieth not; charity vaunteth not itself, is not puffed up.

Doth not behave itself unseemly, seeketh not her own, is not easily provoked, thinketh no evil;

Rejoiceth not in iniquity, but rejoiceth in the truth;

Beareth all things, believeth all things, hopeth all things, endureth all things.

Charity never faileth. . . .

And now abideth faith, hope, charity, these three; but the greatest of these is charity. (13:1–8, 13.)

Sometimes we find it difficult to love our child because of disappointing choices made. And it is almost hard to believe that Christ asks us, today, in the kind of world we live in, to love our enemies. Our little five-year-old grandson pays close attention to his Primary lessons, and they recently talked about loving your enemies. That is a hard concept for a five-year-old. And so he came home from Primary and told his parents that his teacher told him that we have to love our enemies. "Is that true?" he asked. "Do we have to love those bad people who flew their planes into the World Trade Center and killed all those people?"

I believe that love that forgives is an even harder concept for many adults. How do we pray for those that despitefully use us? Where does the Savior ask us to do such a thing as that? It is in Matthew 5:44: "But I say unto you, Love your enemies, bless them that curse you, do good to them that hate you, and pray for them which despitefully use you, and persecute you." I don't know how to do this perfectly, but Christ does. He is the One who had been falsely accused, spat upon, humiliated, scourged, nailed to a cross and, in His agony, said, "Father, forgive them; for they know not what they do" (Luke 23:34).

"Greater love hath no man than this, that a man lay down his life for his friends" (John 15:13). Our precious Savior, our dear Redeemer, gave His life, His whole life, to show us the way; and then He gave up His life for us. He has fulfilled His part of the plan. Now it is up to us to do our part. We must love Him and follow His example, do His work.

We often sing the words from John:

As I have loved you, Love one another.
This new commandment: Love one another.
By this shall men know Ye are my disciples,
If ye have love One to another.[4]

So there you have it. A little formula for finding light at the end of the tunnel, even a light to every corner of our lives: "Have faith, hope, and charity. That's the way to live successfully. How do I know? The Bible tells me so." And, may I add, so do the Book of Mormon and other scriptures, as well as our living prophets.

May we follow the Savior's example and His teachings through the good as well as the hard times in our lives. As we come upon a tunnel in our life's experiences that seems too dark and fearsome, may we be blessed to find our lives and our whole beings filled with that light which "groweth brighter and brighter until the perfect day" (D&C 50:24). May the Savior, that perfect "light and life of the world" (Mosiah 16:9) always beckon you forward; indeed, may His light shine on your path and show you the right way to go forever.

8

Remember the Children

❧

A sacred scene is created in the mind's eye when reading about how the Savior loved and blessed the Nephite children when He came to visit the Saints in the land of Bountiful. After Jesus blessed them, angels surrounded them, one by one, with fire from heaven. I love the account as recorded in 3 Nephi 17:21–24:

> And he took their little children, one by one, and blessed them, and prayed unto the Father for them.
>
> And when he had done this he wept again;
>
> And he spake unto the multitude, and said unto them: Behold your little ones.
>
> And as they looked to behold they cast their eyes

towards heaven, and they saw the heavens open, and they saw angels descending out of heaven as it were in the midst of fire; and they came down and encircled those little ones about, and they were encircled about with fire; and the angels did minister unto them.

Composer Janice Kapp Perry has recorded this account in her tender song, "Remember the Children." Verse one has the following words:

> *Jesus commanded them to bring the children*
> *He took them one by one and gently blessed them.*
> *Angels encircled them with fire from heaven*
> *Then Jesus spoke again, Behold your little ones.*
> *Each one was blessed and Jesus wept.*[1]

Surely He wept from a heart made tender by the innocence and promise of these precious little ones. Oh, that all who minister to little children today could be filled with the same tenderness!

A young mother awoke in the middle of the night troubled about her children. They were all clean and well fed and tucked in after prayers, but something was wrong. She went to her journal to try and record her concerns and get some peace. Among other things, she wrote, "Have I loved the children enough today?"

Statistics and stories we hear today too often show that sometimes those who are responsible for blessing and loving the little ones aren't doing such a good job of it. Child development experts know that much of what a child learns and experiences before the age of five affects the patterns of his life. They confirm what God has taught: "Train up a child in the way he should go: and when he is old, he will not depart from it" (Proverbs 22:6).

I thought of that again recently when attending some stake meetings. A young stake priesthood leader in his early thirties was called from the meeting because of an urgent problem in his family. He was taken not to his home where he'd left his happy young family earlier but to his wife's bedside in the hospital. There, in that same hospital, he had stood vigil over her only a month earlier.

On that earlier day his wife lay precariously close to death after having just delivered their fifth child. But complications with her heart had developed and the outcome looked grim. The doctors told them to prepare for her imminent death. The young mother understood and she pled mightily with the Lord that she might live to go home to her children. You see, she explained to the Lord, she had scolded them and she wanted desperately to assure them of her love, not leave them with any question of her devotion to them. She felt she couldn't leave them with her last cross words ringing in their ears. Her Heavenly Father answered her pleading. She was spared for one month. She went home and loved those children—not indulging them but loving them dearly with hugs and stories and hugs and prayers and smiles and kisses. Following the Saturday chores she and the children played joyously at the community swimming pool while Daddy was at the training meeting, when suddenly she was stricken with a massive heart problem. She collapsed and was rushed to the hospital. Her children were taken dripping wet to grandma's house. And just that suddenly, her earthly mission was ended. But she had been spared to love her children for one more month.

Remember the day that small child was placed in your care? That day a partnership was established between parent and God. He who loves the children so dearly requires a full accounting of that sacred steward-ship. Jesus, who loved the children when He was on the earth and loves them today, asks that we do, too. The song goes on to the chorus with these words:

> *Remember the children*
> *Remember to give them love*
> *Remember to build them*
> *Remember to lift them up*
> *Remember to teach them of plain and*
>   *precious things*
> *Hold them and heal them*
> *Comfort and shield them*
> *Remember the children.*[2]

What an important reminder those words are! As parents we must remember the children in all we do: in decisions we make about *where* to live but more important, *how* to live. Remember the children in decisions regarding marriage and divorce. Remember the children in what we say and how we say it; who we criticize and who we pray for and who we love and how we show our love and who we worship. Remember the children in what we read and watch and laugh at and accept or reject. Remember the children in what we acquire and require and in our priorities. The second verse of the song goes like this:

Jesus commanded us to love the children
And He will stand by us if hearts are
    willing
Then when the world's acclaim
Would pull us from them
We'll hear his voice again
Behold your little ones
Each one still bright with heaven's light
Love them as He did then
Teach them to trust in Him until he
    comes again.
Remember the children.[3]

It is my conviction that our Heavenly Father will strengthen even the weakest of us to remember the children in His way as we seek Him in prayer, learn of His ways by learning His word, and worship Him in our every thought and action. I pray that we all will turn to Him and feel of His love—to make the remembering brighter and more joyful.

9

Mothers Are Leaders

One of the exciting things about traveling to rural Utah in the springtime of the year is to drive through a herd of sheep being moved along the highway and toward their summer home in the mountains. As you come upon a sheep herd, you have to stop the vehicle because it gets swallowed up in the herd. Surrounding you is a moving mass of noisy off-white wool. You almost get dizzy watching the movement and hearing the clanging of sheep bells, the baaing of the sheep, and the frantic bleating of the little lambs. This is accompanied by the barking of dogs as they nip at the heels of the sheep slowly moving down the roadway. Suddenly, as if in a wave, all the animals will scatter to one side as they follow a sheep in the lead, and then you can make some progress down the highway. The sheepherders on horseback are ever present, riding up behind the herd, waving their hats, yelling and whistling as they try to get the herd back on the road and heading in the right direction.

This herd mentality is interesting to observe in sheep and it happens to human beings, too! I remember well a high school principal who came before the student body at the end of an assembly to encourage them to behave differently than usual as they left for lunch. He was very unhappy with past behavior and called all of the teenagers sheep. In fact, his exact words were, "You act just like a herd of sheep, sheep, sheep!" These disgusted words he used turned out to be one of the famous, mocking phrases of the high school students at the school he headed. His statement definitely meant something to the audience in that rural high school!

I knew another principal. When he walked into an assembly of the student body they all rose to their feet and gave this man a standing ovation. It's true! It was a tradition. He would then walk to the podium, where stood the conducting student body president, put his arm about his shoulders, say an encouraging word or two to the assembled students, and then take his place on the front row of the audience. Students in this high school, in a traditionally more rough area of a large city, had great love and respect for their adult leader and for the school property as well. The halls were lined with beautiful original oil paintings and none were ever disturbed or defaced. The student body took pride in their beautiful surroundings.

Why do you think the teenage students loved and respected this principal and this school so much? I believe it was because they were loved by him. Stories were often quietly shared about the silent acts of kindness this good man performed for his students in need: there were new shoes, new coats, and quiet words of encouragement spoken at critical times. There was teaching with love, and a showing of respect for the youth and their building and it was reciprocated in kind by the students as they respected him.

In order to be respected it is important to be respectable. They were blessed with respect from one worthy of respect. They learned, by example, about the Good Shepherd.

There were two leaders—two principals—and one made a positive difference as he led by love and it made all the difference. "He goeth before them and the sheep follow him" (John 10:4).

Today in Israel shepherds still care for sheep the same way they did two thousand years ago when Jesus walked among men. Each evening at sundown, shepherds bring their small flocks of sheep to a common enclosure where they are secured against the wolves and other predators that roam the fields. A single shepherd guards the gate until morning, when the shepherds come to the enclosure one by one and call to their sheep by name. The sheep will not respond to the voice of a stranger but will leave the enclosure only in the care of their true shepherd, confident because the shepherd knows their names and they know his voice.

This is described in John 10:2–5:

> But he that entereth in by the door is the shepherd of the sheep.
>
> To him the porter openeth; and the sheep hear his voice: and he calleth his own sheep by name, and leadeth them out.
>
> And when he putteth forth his own sheep, he goeth before them, and the sheep follow him: for they know his voice.

And a stranger will they not follow, but will flee
from him: for they know not the voice of strangers.

The Savior was the Good Shepherd. Mothers are
shepherds, too, but sometimes we act like sheep
herders. Our charge to lead His sheep requires our
finest efforts in leadership and a lifetime of following
His holy example. Remember the scripture in 1 John
4:19: "We love him, because he first loved us."

Love is the key to opening the door of leadership—
love for those we would lead and love for Him who
loved us first, our Lord and Savior, Jesus Christ.

To lead others, then, one must first be a follower, a
follower of the perfect leader, the Good Shepherd. One
such sister leader blessed my life by her quiet leadership
at a tender time in her life. This is how it happened:

In 1998 we had a wonderful General Young
Women Meeting. It was the first our presidency had
responsibility for. Young women from Holland were
going to receive the broadcast by satellite for the first
time ever, and they wanted to be part of the meeting.
And so they sent tulips and daffodils, two thousand of
them, to add to the beauty of the occasion. It was a
spectacular sight to see all those flowers at the front
of Tabernacle! Following the meeting I gathered an

armful of those beautiful tulips from Holland and took them to the bedside of my friend who was receiving treatment for a serious illness.

When I arrived with the flowers, she was in bed. Two weeks earlier surgeons had removed a large malignant tumor attached to numerous internal organs; however, they were not able to get it all. She had had her first chemotherapy treatment. The sweet, loving attitude always exemplified by this woman was magnified this day. There was no bitterness toward a doctor who had been unwilling to explore her health concerns for several years, thereby leaving the cancer to grow and overtake her system—only an expression of reliance on the Lord and how she had felt on a day she described to me when she knew she was filled with the spirit of the Holy Ghost. Her question: "Why, when it is so magnificent, don't we live to have that Spirit with us constantly?" Her question led me home to ponder the blessings of the Spirit.

From her bed she led me, led me closer to heaven. Thank you, Sister Bush. As a follower of Christ she was a powerful leader. In the quiet peace of her testimony I saw the hand of God at work.

When we draw close to Him, He can work through each of us no matter what our individual situations are.

There are calls for leadership all around us in today's world: especially in our homes, but also in our communities, schools, church, and workplace. I believe that all women today have some responsibility to be leaders. It is not sufficient, nor is it acceptable, for us to think that what we say and what we do doesn't really matter. In today's world, we do not have the luxury of saying that we will let someone else do it, or that we are too busy, or we don't know how, or we aren't interested, or let the men do it. We must all realize that, like it or not, we have been given a leadership responsibility by virtue of living in this time and season of the world's history. That's a very awesome and daunting idea, isn't it? But I believe it is true.

So did President Spencer W. Kimball. Speaking to the women of the Church, he said, "Much of the major growth that is coming to the Church in the last days will come because many of the good women of the world . . . will be drawn to the Church in large numbers. This will happen to the degree that the women of the Church reflect righteousness and articulateness in their lives and to the degree that they are seen as distinct and different—in happy ways—from the women of the world."[1]

I believe that today's women can use their God-given abilities to motivate, inspire, manage, and build. Whether paid or volunteer, women's leadership talents can, and will, and must bless the world! And I believe that as we assume this leadership responsibility we will be blessed and magnified, and the world in which we live will be better for our having been there.

I hardly considered myself a leader when I was knee-deep in diapers and motherhood. Do you consider yourself a leader? Let me share excerpts from my journal that capture the essence of life in those busy family times:

> Five A.M. and I'm awake as usual. Can't seem to sleep past four A.M. these past several weeks. There is a great deal of movement with the twins that I am carrying plus I wake up and think about a myriad of things: finishing the basement; where to sleep all the children; better get a new nightgown for the hospital and fix the zipper in my robe; how will I raise all these children; have I loved the children enough today; are we making progress with the 4th child; does his stomach protrude abnormally; how can I

keep up this big house; will I need to be released from my church callings; will I ever have a satisfying calling again; what about a kitchen table and chairs to seat nine; and on and on. And the tenor of the times is bad. Russia has its heaviest troops poised on Poland's boarder; Pres. Reagan is in the hospital recovering from a bullet wound to his left chest; a would-be assassin shot him and three others in his company March 30. General conference was last weekend with endless warnings about living within our means and having a year's supply of money and food. And today I have to go withdraw from our savings to pay for beds we need and the construction of the basement. We all should see the dentist, and the baby chicks we got for Easter are dying, and I feel bad for our little boys who have to bury them. You can see that I feel like my life is in a state of confusion and peace is preferred. Getting closer to the Lord will help. I know that. Then I'm so slow physically—can't accomplish as much as fast. My big question: what kind of woman will emerge from this in 10 years? What kind of children?

Women have so many worries! When I was right in the thick of my mothering responsibilities, I had seven young boys and a very busy husband. I just remember trying to manage our home, and teach piano lessons, and have church jobs, and serve on committees in the community, and keep up with the lives of each of the children. One particular day I felt very overwhelmed! At this time my husband was the director of the MBA program at Brigham Young University. In frustration I called him on the phone and said, "This job is too much for me. I can't figure it out. Why don't you bring a team of those bright MBA students over here and see if they can figure out how to run a home smoothly with the kind of life we live?"

We joked about it, and I hung up the phone feeling better. But I often wondered if those students with their specialized training would really know how to meet the demands placed on a mother.

Once I heard my husband speaking with someone and he commented, "You know, I have been the CEO of a company; I have taught management to graduate students; I have been the president of a university; I have bought and sold real estate; and I have served with a variety of boards of directors. But the toughest negotiating I've ever done has been with my own teenage children."

Can you relate to those feelings of a parent? It takes leadership skills to be a parent!

To be most effective and make the best use of her talents, a woman must learn the skill of prioritizing. She will learn to discern those things which matter most and give them top priority. There will be things only she can do well. There will be things that she can delegate. There will be things that she can do later. There will be things that she must do now. In her leadership roles, today's woman will see that there will be things that matter most and things that matter least. The great leaders will be patient women and they will come to realize, sooner or later, that "out of small things proceedeth that which is great" (D&C 64:33).

President James E. Faust said it well at the General Young Women Meeting held March 28, 1998: "However, you cannot do all these things well at the same time. You cannot eat all of the pastries in the baking shop at once. You will get a tummyache. You cannot be a 100-percent wife, a 100-percent mother, a 100-percent Church worker, a 100-percent career person, and a 100-percent public-service person at the same time. How can all of these roles be coordinated? I suggest that you can have it sequentially."[2]

I would like to focus on four qualities innate in women, in mothers, which make them great leaders.

Women are good listeners. A young woman described so well her mother's ability to listen.

> I would come home from school and see Mom in the kitchen simmering chili. I would open the refrigerator, close it, and say, "Why don't we ever have anything good to eat?"
>
> Then I would go downstairs, take off my sweater, throw it on the floor, come upstairs, open the refrigerator door again, and say, "What's for dinner?" Mom would tell me. "Ugh," I would say. "We just had that."
>
> Then I would call my best friend and be told that she was at a yearbook meeting. I would walk around the living room, pick up a magazine, throw it on the sofa, go into the kitchen again, and open the refrigerator. I would tell my mother that I did not want a nice, fresh apple. Then I would heave an enormous sigh, look in the cupboards, leave them open, listen to Mom ask if there was anything wrong, and tell her, "No." I would go downstairs, bang on the piano, have an argument with a sibling, come upstairs and look in the refrigerator, shut it

again, and agree to chop the green peppers for Mom.

Then—observing her still simmering chili on the stove—I would sit down on a stool and say, "You know that stupid Tommy Morgan? I hate that stupid Tommy Morgan!"

Then Mom, not looking up from the chili (most moms knew you'd stop talking if they looked up from the chili) would say, "Oh, really? Why do you feel that way?" And somewhere between chopping the green peppers and running the dishwasher, I would tell her.[3]

Women are compassionate and nurturing by nature. An example of this is the story of Sally Bush.

She was sometimes called Sally, a widow with three children. Perhaps life had been a little harsh and she would have welcomed a change for the better, the easier, if it came. She thought she saw it come when a man, a widower from her past, returned with a proposal of marriage in his nice suit of clothes and talk of a prosperous farm. The prospects of a better life grew, and she understood him to mention servants and to be a man of substance. She accepted and crossed the river with him to view her new possessions: A farm grown up to wild blackberry vines and sumac, a floorless, windowless hut, the only servants were two thinly clad barefoot children, the father of whom had borrowed the suit and the boots that he had gone a-courting in. Her first thought was the obvious one: go back home. But she looked at the children, especially the younger, a boy whose melancholy gaze met hers. For a moment she looked while a great spirit subdued the passions of the flesh and then, rolling up her sleeves, she quietly spoke immortal words which ought to be engraven on every parent or teacher's heart: "I'll stay for the sake of this boy."

"Oh, Sally Bush, what a treasure trembled in the balance that day," wrote one whose mother was a neighbor of the boy. And Sally Bush didn't know, when she looked at that melancholy face of ten years, that her stepson would someday save this nation, heal a generational breech, and become the immortal Abraham Lincoln. She uttered what should be engraven on every parent or teacher's heart, "I'll stay for the sake of this boy."[4]

Women have a unique point of view, not always like that of a man. Our priesthood leaders understand this. They value the difference and seek our input. For this reason they are emphasizing the council system in the Church and in families and asking sister leaders to speak up, to participate in meaningful ways. Priesthood leaders know the benefits of all leaders, men and women, working together to solve problems. President Boyd K. Packer taught this concept in April 1998 general conference when he said, "To the degree that leaders ignore the contribution and influence of these sisters, in councils and in the home, the work of the priesthood itself is limited and weakened."[5]

That gives us, as women, the responsibility to communicate clearly, kindly, helpfully, and responsibly. For example, an effective auxiliary leader could say to her priesthood leader: "I have three concerns in our program. They are: One, two, three. I have some recommendations after counseling with the presidency and advisors. They are: One, two, three." Sister leaders can make a unique and wonderful difference if they will speak up and address an issue from their perspective using clear communication techniques.

In families, when discussing matters in family councils or even more informally, mothers can make a difference when they address an issue from their feminine point of view, with all the goodness and insight that is part of their nature. Add to this a determination to communicate the issue clearly, not confusing her children or her husband with too many details or side stories. It seems that men like to hear the theme of the symphony, not the whole symphony!

Women are influential. They have greater influence than they know. There is no one who can set a standard for the family better than the mother. Her influence is born of gentleness and love and that special intuition given to women. Today we need mothers to exert their influence for modesty in a world where that is becoming a scarce commodity. We need mothers who exhibit modesty in speech and in action and in appearance and who then encourage that in their children.

Mothers can have a most positive effect on their daughters, as I have seen firsthand. You may know that I am the mother of seven sons. I know boys! It has been an exciting life at our house. I've learned a lot from them and from their friends, both boys and girls. I remember the time one of them had a date for the prom. He brought her to our home before the dance so we could take pictures. When they got there he came into the kitchen, where I was looking for the camera, and said, "Wait until you see Kelly's dress. She looks so beautiful!" Adam had never said anything like that before so I could hardly wait to see what he meant.

When I saw her I understood; she was lovely. The dress she was wearing was beautiful; I learned that she and her mother had searched everywhere for it. When they finally found this dress, they knew it would be perfect with some added fabric and finishing touches to meet their high standards.

All their efforts were rewarded because she was absolutely radiant that night, but it was more than the dress that made her shine. It was her quiet confidence. As I looked at her, I was reminded of the scripture, "Let virtue garnish thy thoughts unceasingly; then shall thy confidence wax strong" (D&C 121:45). Mothers can help their children have that kind of confidence as they exert their gentle leadership and help them do what is right.

Dear, wonderful mother, can you catch a vision of yourself as a leader? When you step up as an example of love and caring and covenant-keeping you are exerting your influence for good and it is more powerful than you may know!

It is a blessing to know that the children who come under the refining influence of mothers are the magnificent creations of God Himself. Before the world was, they were prepared to come forth in this day and to come under our influence. When you lead them in your role as a mother, you must know first of all that the only way to lead them or guide them or to ever walk beside them in any meaningful measure is to first be a follower of Jesus Christ, to be His undershepherd. For each of us to be His devoted disciple and to respond to His invitation to "come, follow me" provides the way for us to bless their lives and be a masterful mother-leader.

"Wherefore, be not weary in well-doing, for ye are laying the foundation of a great work. And out of small things proceedeth that which is great" (D&C 64:33).

10

Be Yours to Hold It High

I have never forgotten my visit to the American War Cemetery in England. Buried there are thousands of young men from the United States who gave their lives on foreign soil in defense of freedom. These young soldiers were the best blood of their generation and, tragically, they had been claimed by the horrors of war. As we looked out across acres of green grass covered by thousands of white crosses that marked the graves of these soldiers, our attention was drawn to the flag flying over this sacred spot. At the base of the flagpole these words were inscribed: "To you from failing hands we throw the torch; be yours to hold it high."[1]

The torch—a symbol of courage and faith—was

passed from these hands to those able to live and carry on.

You, a mother, are the noblest of torchbearers. And you pass the torch from your hands to the outstretched hands of your children and succeeding generations.

Each of us has been handed a torch, the gospel torch that lights the path to true freedom in the kingdom of God for every soul on earth. When hands were laid upon your head and you were confirmed a member of The Church of Jesus Christ, you were, in essence, being given a gospel torch and asked to hold it high, to shed its light along the path for those who walk in darkness. It's exciting work you've been called to do! And you are just the ones to do it. You are the best blood of your generation, and the Lord is counting on you to help bring true freedom to the earth, the freedom that only the gospel of Jesus Christ can offer mankind.

As I stood there that day reading those impressive words—"To you from failing hands we throw the torch; be yours to hold it high"—my mind went to the great prophet Moroni. I could just picture him writing his last words on the plates and then burying them up, knowing that one day, in the due time of the Lord, they would be brought forth to bless God's children, like a torch to light the way. Listen to his lonely and poignant words as he wrote on the sacred and precious records of his fathers for the last time:

> Behold I, Moroni, do finish the record of my father, Mormon. Behold, I have but few things to write, which things I have been commanded by my father.
>
> And now it came to pass that after the great and tremendous battle at Cumorah, behold, the Nephites who had escaped into the country southward were hunted by the Lamanites, until they were all destroyed.
>
> And my father also was killed by them, and I even remain alone to write the sad tale of the destruction of my people. But behold, they are gone, and I fulfil the commandment of my father. And whether they will slay me, I know not.
>
> Therefore I will write and hide up the records in the earth; and whither I go it mattereth not (Mormon 8:1–4).

Doesn't that sound to you a little bit like, "To you from failing hands I throw the torch?"

Now listen to the next part, because he prophesied that this great sacred record that was hidden up would again come forth. He says, "And blessed be he that shall bring this thing to light; for it shall be brought out of darkness unto light, according to the word of God; yea, it shall be brought out of the earth, and it shall shine forth out of the darkness, and come unto the knowledge of the people; and it shall be done by the power of God" (Mormon 8:16).

That is the part about "Be yours to hold it high." This great record, the Book of Mormon, was preserved and brought forth by the power of a loving Father in Heaven to bless and guide the lives of His children in these latter days. It is like a torch. You, and I, have been called to share it with others, to hold its teachings out for others to see. The Book of Mormon has the power to change lives, to give them direction, to inspire, to teach, to build faith. Its words shed light on my understanding of the gospel every time I read from its pages. How grateful I am for it!

As you read and study the gospel and the Book of Mormon, you will see the flame of your torch growing brighter. As you determine to live the commandments of God with exactness and honor you will be a guide and a light to others. Your family and associates will be blessed because of your good example. Others will sense a special spirit and light that you will radiate. The spirit will work through you to touch hearts. Your understanding will deepen and increase because your spirit will be receptive.

Let me share with you an example of the importance of one little light in the darkness. It was just a few days before Christmas and we were a newly married couple, expecting our first child, and traveling home for the Christmas holidays. It was a long trip (forty-two hours driving) from Boston to home; but we were eager, especially me, to come home for Christmas. So we filled the car with friends who would help pay for the gas and take turns driving, and headed for home. Oh, there truly is no place like home for the holidays, and our spirits were high in anticipation of being reunited with loved ones again! We were about two-thirds of the way home, going through the plains of Nebraska, when we drove into a blinding blizzard of snow blowing and billowing and growing deeper and deeper on the highway with each passing moment. The night was pure black, and the storm was absolutely fierce. Before long we were trying to plow through at least a foot of snow as we crept along the freeway. We couldn't see the lines of the road and couldn't see where we were going. This was literally a blinding snowstorm. Suddenly in front of us there appeared a huge semi-truck going slowly and steadily ahead. We could barely make out his small red taillights, but seeing them gave us hope. My husband, who was the driver, fixed his eyes on the small lights from the truck and then we drove along in the tracks he made through the deepening snow. Our panic subsided somewhat with that guide up ahead because we knew of his experience and expertise in driving the highways. He knew the route, and he sat up higher in his rig and could perhaps have a better view, and surely he was equipped with radio equipment whereby he could get some help from others who were ahead of us down the road.

With prayers on our lips and white-knuckled hands holding on, we followed our unsuspecting leader through the storm. We passed many cars that had swerved off onto the sides of the road, but we kept moving slowly forward. Before long we could sense that the semi was slowing down and pulling off the roadway. We followed him and soon found ourselves safely in the parking lot of what looked to be an overcrowded motel. We were to a place of refuge and we were so very, very grateful. We all hurried inside and got the last room in the place. We found the truck driver and thanked him profusely for leading us to safety.

Times will come, if they haven't already, when you will be at some situation or place in life where someone you know will be in the middle of a blizzard. It won't be a snowstorm like we experienced, but it will be a storm even more dangerous to their souls. They will be looking for a way to safety. Your light, the light from your little torch, can guide them to safety within the kingdom of God. How very much better that will be than the overcrowded motel where we found refuge!

Perhaps the one who will be following your light will be your child; maybe it will be another of your loved ones, or a friend. Who can tell whose life or how many lives you will bless? Perhaps one day you will find that you are an answer to someone's prayer. Will your torch be burning bright enough for that person to see your light?

Let me share with you the story about Mettie Marie Kjar who lived in Denmark. She dreamed one night about a new religion, and it all seemed so real that she awakened her husband and told him about it. She arose from her bed and went to tell her brother about it. She said, "We will join that church." The family record says that her brother seemed a bit upset about it.

Some time later, early one morning as her husband was making the fire, two young Mormon missionaries knocked on their door. They came in and talked to him and gave him a Book of Mormon.

Mettie Marie's husband took the book into the bedroom and told her that here was her new religion. They were both greatly impressed and felt that it was the right church. The light of the gospel touched their hearts and soon a testimony of the gospel burned so strongly in their souls that they could not deny the truthfulness of it. They were baptized at great personal sacrifice. So was her brother and his family. I am eternally and forever grateful for those two missionaries, for Mettie Marie and her husband, Lars Christian Kjar, are my great-great-grandparents.

The light that they followed all those years ago still burns brightly in my heart and soul. And the torch that was kindled in Denmark all those years ago has continued to burn from one generation to the next and has been carried by their posterity to nearly every corner of the earth. Who could count the lives that have been affected, the other torches that have been lit from the first contact from those faithful missionaries with a Book of Mormon on a cold, early winter morning far, far from home?

On a day when it is hard to take time for prayers, to serve your family, to study your scriptures, to hold family home evening, to go on a discouraging errand to serve the Lord, will you pause for just a moment and listen to someone, maybe even Moroni, whispering to you down from the ages: "To you from failing hands we throw the torch; be yours to hold it high"?

And then will you determine to study just a little harder, to pray a little longer, to exercise just a little more faith, to be a little more patient, to hold your torch just a little higher? For it just may be that your child will be trying to follow your light. I pray that you will come to know the literal meaning of the grand scripture in 1 Nephi 17:13:

"And I will also be your light in the wilderness; and I will prepare the way before you, if it so be that ye shall keep my commandments; wherefore, inasmuch as ye shall keep my commandments ye shall be led towards the promised land; and ye shall know that it is by me that ye are led."

The Lord is our light and our salvation. I know that

only through Him and by Him can we and our children come home again to live with our Father in Heaven. I love the light He gives to my little torch. May you and I never let that sacred flame which we have been given die, but rather hold it high and be a light to others.

11

Families: The Wellspring of Society

Mothers can rejoice in the knowledge that it a great blessing to be a daughter of God. What a joy to be a woman alive on the earth in this day and time when we have the fulness of the gospel of Jesus Christ! We are blessed to have the priesthood of God restored to the earth. We are led by a living prophet of God.

For Such a Time as This

I am inspired by the lives of good and faithful women who understand their part in God's plan. Our Heavenly Father loves His daughters very much. From the beginning of time the Lord has placed significant trust in them. He has sent us to earth for such a time as this to perform a grand and glorious mission. The Doctrine and Covenants teaches: "Even before they were born, they, with many others, received their first lessons in the world of spirits and were prepared to come forth in the due time of the Lord to labor in his vineyard for the salvation of the souls of men" (D&C 138:56). What a wonderful vision that gives us of our purpose on earth.

Where much is given, much is required. Our Heavenly Father asks His daughters to walk in virtue, to live in righteousness, so that we can fulfill our life's mission and His purposes. He wants us to be successful and He will help us as we seek His help.

That women were born into this earth female was determined long before mortal birth, as were the divine differences of male and female. I love the clarity of the teachings of the First Presidency and the Quorum of the Twelve in the Proclamation on the Family. They state: "Gender is an essential characteristic of individual premortal, mortal, and eternal identity and purpose."[1] From that statement we are taught that every girl was feminine and female in spirit long before her mortal birth.

God sent women to earth with some qualities in

extra capacity. President James E. Faust observed that femininity "is the divine adornment of humanity. It finds expression in your . . . capacity to love, your spirituality, delicacy, radiance, sensitivity, creativity, charm, graciousness, gentleness, dignity, and quiet strength. It is manifest differently in each girl or woman, but each . . . possesses it. Femininity is part of your inner beauty."[2]

Our outward appearance is a reflection of what we are inside. Our lives reflect that for which we seek. If with all our hearts we truly seek to know the Savior and be more like Him, we shall be, for He is our divine, eternal Brother. But He is more than that. He is our precious Savior, our dear Redeemer. We ask with Alma of old, "Have ye received his image in your countenances?" (Alma 5:14).

Grateful Daughters of God

You can recognize women who are grateful to be daughters of God by their outward appearance. These women understand their stewardship over their bodies and treat them with dignity. They care for their bodies as they would a holy temple for they understand the Lord's teaching: "Know ye not that ye are the temple of God, and that the Spirit of God dwelleth in you?" (1 Corinthians 3:16). Women who love God would never abuse or deface a temple with graffiti. Nor would they throw open the doors of that holy, dedicated edifice and invite the world to look on. How even more sacred is the body, for it was not made by man. It was created by God. We are the stewards, the keepers of the cleanliness and purity with which it came from heaven. "If any man defile the temple of God, him shall God destroy; for the temple of God is holy, which temple ye are" (1 Corinthians 3:17).

Grateful daughters of God guard their bodies carefully for they know they are the wellspring of life and they reverence life. They don't uncover their bodies to find favor with the world. They walk in modesty to be in favor with their Father in Heaven. They know He loves them dearly.

You can recognize women who are grateful to be daughters of God by their attitude. They know that the errand of angels is given to women, and they desire to be on God's errand to love His children and minister to them; to teach them the doctrines of salvation; to call them to repentance; to save them in perilous circumstances; to guide them in the performance of His work;

to deliver His messages. They understand that they can bless their Father's children in their homes and neighborhoods and beyond. Women who are grateful to be daughters of God bring glory to His name.

You can recognize women who are grateful to be daughters of God by their abilities. They fulfill their divine potential and magnify their God-given gifts. They are capable, strong women who bless families, serve others, and understand that the glory of God is intelligence. They are women who embrace enduring virtues in order to be all that our Father needs them to be. The prophet Jacob spoke of some of those virtues when he said their "feelings are exceedingly tender and chaste and delicate before God, which thing is pleasing unto God" (Jacob 2:7).

You can recognize women who are grateful to be daughters of God by their reverence for motherhood, even when that blessing has been withheld from them for a time. In those circumstances, their righteous influence can be a blessing in the lives of children they love. Their exemplary teaching can echo the voice of a faithful home and resonate truth in the hearts of children who need another witness.

Grateful daughters of God love Him and teach their

children to love Him without reservation and without resentment. They are like the mothers of Helaman's youthful army, who had great faith and "had been taught by their mothers, that if they did not doubt, God would deliver them" (Alma 56:47).

When you observe a kind and gentle mother in action, you see a woman of great strength. Her family can feel a spirit of love and respect and safety when they are near her as she seeks the companionship of the Holy Ghost and the guidance of His Spirit. They are blessed by her wisdom and good judgment. The husband and children, whose lives she blesses, will contribute to the stability of societies all over this world. Grateful daughters of God learn truths from their mothers and grandmothers. They teach their daughters the joyful art of creating a home. They seek fine educations for their children and have a thirst for knowledge themselves. They help their children develop skills they can use in serving others. They know that the way they have chosen is not the easy way, but they know it is absolutely worth their finest efforts.

They understand what Elder Neal A. Maxwell meant as he said: "When the real history of mankind is fully disclosed, will it feature the echoes of gunfire or the shaping sound of lullabies? The great armistices made by military men or the peacemaking of women in homes and in neighborhoods? Will what happened in cradles and kitchens prove to be more controlling than what happened in congresses?"[3]

Daughters of God know that it is the nurturing nature of women that can bring everlasting blessings, and they live to cultivate this divine attribute. Surely when a woman reverences motherhood, her children will "arise up, and call her blessed" (Proverbs 31:28).

Women of God cannot be like women of the world. The world has enough women who are tough; we need women who are tender. There are enough women who are coarse; we need women who are kind. There are enough women who are rude; we need women who are refined. We have enough women of fame and fortune; we need more women of faith. We have enough greed; we need more goodness. We have enough vanity; we need more virtue. We have enough popularity; we need more purity.

Keeper of the Springs

And what a privilege it is to be united with so many good women of God, women who are making an effort to maintain and preserve the traditional family as the basic unit of society! I am grateful for the six million women and young women all over this world who belong to the Church and who believe that strong families will produce strong societies and a hopeful future.

I loved my five-year assignment as president of Young Women where we focused our attention on our teenage girls who live in every part of the world. I love them and have great faith in their abilities and in their future. Their future is the future of the world, for they will nurture the generations yet unborn. With you, their mothers, I am concerned about what these girls and their male counterparts hear, read in print, and see acted out on screen. We all know that the media has the power to condone, even promote, anti-family messages by what they print, what they show, and how they show it. There are those who would have us choose abortion over babies, fully-employed women over motherhood, and in place of parents, government-sponsored day care and after-school programs to watch over what they term "burdensome" children.

I believe that youth must be taught that this is wrong. We must teach the ideal; that is, that human life is sacred; that children need mothers to nurture, nourish, and teach them; and that they need fathers to love them, to provide for them, and to protect the family unit as is taught by the First Presidency and the Quorum of the Twelve Apostles in "The Family: A Proclamation to the World."

For those who would believe that the traditional family can be improved on and that a more modern way of doing things is better, may I share a story told by Dr. Peter Marshall, who served for several years as chaplain of the United States Senate:

> Once upon a time there was a town nestled at the foot of a mountain range where it was sheltered from wind and storms. High up in the hills above the little village, a quiet forest dweller took it upon himself to be the Keeper of the Springs.
>
> He patrolled the hills and wherever he found a spring he cleaned its brown pool of silt and fallen leaves of mud and mold and took away from the spring all foreign matter so that the water which bubbled up through the sand ran down clean and cold and pure.
>
> But the City Council was a group of hardheaded, hard-boiled businessmen. They scanned the

civic budget and found in it the salary of the Keeper of the Springs.

Said the Keeper of the Purse: "Why should we pay this romance ranger? We never see him; he is not necessary to our town's work life. If we build a reservoir just above the town, we can dispense with his services and save his salary."

Therefore, the City Council voted to dispense with the unnecessary cost of the Keeper of the Springs and to build a cement reservoir.

So the Keeper of the Springs no longer visited the brown pools but watched from the heights while they built the reservoir.

When it was finished it soon filled up with water to be sure, but the water did not seem to be the same. It did not seem to be as clean, and a green scum soon befouled its stagnant surface.

There were constant troubles with the delicate machinery of the mills, for it was often clogged with slime, and the swans found another home above the town.

At last, an epidemic raged, and the clammy, yellow fingers of sickness reached every home in every street and lane.

The City Council met again. Sorrowfully, it faced

the city's plight, and frankly it acknowledged the mistake of the dismissal of the Keeper of the Springs.

They sought him out high in the hills and begged him to return to his former joyous labor. Gladly he agreed, and began once more to make his rounds. It was not long until pure water came lilting down under tunnels of ferns and mosses and to sparkle in the cleansed reservoir.[4]

There will always be a need for the Keeper of the Springs! The wellsprings of which I speak are the families of this world. In many ways, the homes and families of our world are being more polluted than the mountain springs of the story.

The clammy yellow fingers of moral sickness will reach into every home, every street, and every life unless we are vigilant and proactive.

We must rally this day and in all the days to come to keep the headwaters of the family clear and clean, so that strong, safe, productive boys and girls and men and women may flow freely from them. I honor you for being true to that noble errand to guard your own home and family and then to be an influence in your larger community. I would like to offer three suggestions for being Keepers of the Springs.

First, we must teach and model traditional family values. The solutions offered by some, like the reservoir of the story, cannot substitute for the daily, individual attention given by parents who are willing to invest their best time and efforts. We must teach and model that happiness and security comes in families with a father and mother who are married and committed to each other, committed to nurturing children and raising them to be caring, productive adults.

May women—accomplished, capable, well-educated women—never apologize for following the traditions that have made our society strong. Make those traditions of vigilant watchcare over home and family your number one priority. May our daughters aspire to noble motherhood as their greatest calling and not succumb to the demeaning alternative voices of those who would destroy families.

May men of learning and understanding and influence stand prepared to fulfill their duties as provider and protector in the family setting. May we teach our sons to embrace their position of responsibility in future families.

May we believe and then teach that marriage between a man and a woman and fidelity in that marriage is the truest safeguard for home and family. Recent data from the Research Division of the LDS Church show that those in the Church who practice these principles experience a divorce rate one-fifth of the U.S. average.

Second, we must teach and model moral values. There is no viable substitute for the traditional moral values that keep families strong. Encourage youth to develop religious faith, acquire a fine education, understand the relationship between choice and accountability, do good works, and live lives of integrity. They must know that they are responsible for the nurture and stability of future families, not governments or agencies.

No society ever became great by lowering its moral standards. Politically correct is not always morally correct! We need Keepers of the Springs who will realize that what is socially acceptable in our world today may not be morally right. To be great, we must be good!

Third, we must use our influence. I honor you for being true to that noble errand to guard your own homes and families and then to be an influence in your larger community. If Keepers of the Springs desert their posts or are unfaithful to their responsibilities, the future outlook for this world is bleak indeed. How large will your sphere of influence be and how far will it reach? You decide. It is up to you.

I believe in the importance of the traditional family as the ideal. My own experience convinces me of the supreme value of this ideal. Let me show you the evidence I have.

For thirty years I have devoted my life to this family. How grateful I am for the blessing and opportunity to be a keeper of one little spring. With all that I could have chosen to do, with whatever ability and talent I have, I doubt that anything else I could have chosen could have more long-term impact in our society than these seven sons who have been scattered across this world from Russia to Wall Street, Africa to England, Guatemala to Germany, Belgium to Brazil, doing good for mankind.

Now these seven sons, products of our family, are getting married, producing incomes, and becoming fathers. They are establishing traditional families of their own and a new generation of Keepers of the Springs is beginning.

In my own experience, limited as it may be, I believe that it is in the family where your sons and your daughters and where our boys and their wives will find their greatest satisfaction, their fulfillment, their peace, their joy, and their intergenerational influence.

As creators and defenders of the family, we, as mothers, are involved in something everlasting.

I believe our influence will live on through our sons and our daughters, those we touch on a daily basis and subsequent generations. They will bless many lives and, in the end, they will bless our lives because each of us was a Keeper of the Springs.

Notes

Notes to Chapter 1: A Woman of Faith

1. M. Russell Ballard, "The Greatest Generation of Missionaries," *Ensign,* November 2002, 46.
2. See Gordon B. Hinckley, "Women of the Church," *Ensign,* November 1996, 69.

Notes to Chapter 2: The Family— How Firm a Foundation

1. "How Firm a Foundation," *Hymns of The Church of Jesus Christ of Latter-day Saints* (Salt Lake City: Intellectual Reserve, Inc., 1985), no. 85.
2. Sheila Hotchkin, "N. J. City Sets Aside a Family Night," *Deseret News,* March 25, 2002, A2.
3. Dick Feagler, "All Time Spent with Child Is Quality," *Deseret News,* May 22, 1997, A27.
4. Gordon B. Hinckley, *Teachings of Gordon B. Hinckley* (Salt Lake City: Deseret Book, 1997), 213–14.
5. Harold B. Lee, "Maintain Your Place As a Woman," *Ensign,* February 1972, 51.

6. Orson F. Whitney, in Conference Report, April 29, 110.
7. "How Firm a Foundation," *Hymns,* no. 85.

Notes to Chapter 3: The Desire of Your Heart

1. Jeffrey R. Holland, *On Earth As It Is in Heaven* (Salt Lake City: Deseret Book, 1989), 210–12.
2. Gordon B. Hinckley, *The Wondrous and True Story of Christmas,* booklet (Salt Lake City: Deseret Book, 2003), 5–7.
3. Melvin J. Ballard, *Melvin J. Ballard—Crusader for Righteousness* (Salt Lake City: Bookcraft, 1966), 65–66.

Notes to Chapter 4: That Our Children May Know to What Source They May Look

1. Boyd K. Packer, "Little Children," *Ensign,* November 1986, 17.
2. J. Reuben Clark, "First Presidency Sets Standards for Church Educators," in James R. Clark, comp., *Messages of the First Presidency,* 6 vols. (Salt Lake City: Bookcraft, 1965–75), 6:47, 54.
3. Jay Evensen, "Religion Can Combat a Parent's Worst Nightmare," *Deseret News,* April 9, 2000, AA1.
4. Packer, "Little Children," *Ensign,* November 1986, 17.
5. Gordon B. Hinckley, *Teachings of Gordon B. Hinckley* (Salt Lake City: Deseret Book, 1997), 311.
6. "The Family: A Proclamation to the World," *Ensign,* November 1995, 102.
7. Ibid.
8. Hinckley, *Teachings,* 523–24.
9. *For the Strength of Youth,* pamphlet (Salt Lake City: The Church of Jesus Christ of Latter-day Saints, 2001), 2–3.
10. See similar version of story in Stephen D. Nadauld, *Principles of Priesthood Leadership* (Salt Lake City: Bookcraft, 1999), 76–78.
11. Ibid.

12. See Brent Top and Bruce Chadwick, *Rearing Righteous Youth of Zion: Great News, Good News, and Not-So-Good News* (Salt Lake City: Bookcraft, 1998).

Notes to Chapter 5: Fathers

1. "The Family: A Proclamation to the World," *Ensign,* November 1995, 102.
2. In Amy Donaldson, "Seljaas Is 2002 Ms. Basketball," *Deseret News,* March 12, 2002, D1.

Note to Chapter 6: Of One Heart

1. Mary A. Pepper Kidder, "Did You Think to Pray?" *Hymns of The Church of Jesus Christ of Latter-day Saints* (Salt Lake City: Intellectual Reserve, Inc., 1985), no. 140.

Notes to Chapter 7: The Light at the End of the Tunnel

1. Don Cecil Corbett, *Mary Fielding Smith, Daughter of Britain: Portrait of Courage* (Salt Lake City: Deseret Book, 1966), 236–37.
2. David O. McKay in *Relief Society Magazine,* January 1948, 8.
3. Boyd K. Packer, *The Holy Temple* (Salt Lake City: Bookcraft, 1980), 183–85.
4. Luacine Clark Fox, "Love One Another," *Hymns of The Church of Jesus Christ of Latter-day Saints* (Salt Lake City: Intellectual Reserve, Inc., 1985), no. 308.

Notes to Chapter 8: Remember the Children

1. Janice Kapp Perry, "Remember the Children," from *In the Arms of His Love,* sound recording (Provo: Prime Recordings, 1992).
2. Ibid.
3. Ibid.

Notes to Chapter 9: Mothers Are Leaders

1. Spencer W. Kimball, *My Beloved Sisters* (Salt Lake City: Deseret Book, 1979), 44.
2. James E. Faust, "How Near to the Angels," *Ensign*, May 1998, 95.
3. Linda Burton, *What's a Smart Woman Like You Doing at Home?* Rev. ed. (Vienna, Virginia: Mothers at Home, 1992).
4. In Jeffrey R. Holland, "That Our Children May Know . . . " *1981 Fireside and Devotional Speeches* (Provo: Brigham Young University Press, 1981), 158.
5. Boyd K. Packer, "The Relief Society," *Ensign*, May 1998, 72.

Note to Chapter 10: Be Yours to Hold It High

1. John McCrae, "In Flanders Field," in *The Best-Loved Poems of the American People* (Garden City, New Jersey: Doubleday & Co., Inc., 1936), 429.

Notes to Chapter 11: Families: The Wellspring of Society

1. "The Family: A Proclamation to the World," *Ensign*, November 1995, 102.
2. James E. Faust, "Womanhood: The Highest Place of Honor," *Ensign*, May 2000, 96.
3. Neal A. Maxwell, "The Women of God," *Ensign*, May 1978, 10–11.
4. Peter Marshall, *Keeper of the Springs and Other Messages from "Mister Jones, Meet the Master"* (Westwood, New York: Fleming H. Revell Co., 1962), 9–11.

Index

Index